THE ROMANTIC POETS

English Literature

Editor

PROFESSOR JOHN LAWLOR
MA
Professor of English in the University of Keele

THE ROMANTIC POETS

Graham Hough

Professor of English
in the University of Cambridge

HUTCHINSON UNIVERSITY LIBRARY
LONDON

HUTCHINSON & CO *(Publishers)* LTD
178-202 Great Portland Street, London W1

London   Melbourne   Sydney
Auckland   Johannesburg
Cape Town

First published 1953
Second edition 1957
Reprinted 1958, 1960, 1963 and 1965
Third edition 1967
Reprinted 1968, 1970

Cover design of the paperback edition shows The Flight of
Florimel *by Washington Allston by the kind permission
of The Detroit Institute of Arts*

*This book has been set in Imprint, printed in Great Britain
on Smooth Wove paper Offset lithography by Redwood Press of Trowbridge,
and bound by Wm. Brendon, of Tiptree, Essex*
IBSN.   09 040513 7 (cased)
09 040514 5 (paper)

CONTENTS

Preface   vi

I   GRAY   7

II WORDSWORTH AND COLERIDGE

    i The Young Wordsworth   25

    ii The Great Decade   41

    iii Poetic Diction and Imagination 67

    iv Later Years   85

III BYRON   97

IV SHELLEY

    i Shelley and Godwin   122

    ii Prometheus Unbound   133

    iii Shelley as a Lyrist   140

    iv The Defence of Poetry   150

V KEATS

    i The Realm of Flora   156

    ii 'Negative Capability'   169

    iii The Two Hyperions   180

A Short Bibliography   195

Index of Works Discussed   199

PREFACE TO THE THIRD EDITION (1967)

IN looking over work done nearly fifteen years ago one would always like to re-write it. Since this was not practicable I have added a short up-to-date bibliography giving a guide to the most important recent work, as well as to the older editions and studies.

November 1966   G.H.

PREFACE TO THE SECOND EDITION (1957)

I SHOULD have liked to re-write the book at much greater length. Since this is not possible, I have added to the "Suggestions for Further Reading" and a little to the notes. A few mistakes have also been corrected, and a page or so added to the Wordsworth and Coleridge chapter.

PREFACE TO THE FIRST EDITION (1953)

THE object of this small book is to give a critical survey of the work of the major Romantic poets. By way of introduction, I have added a chapter on Gray. The main difficulty has been one of compression; so I have kept strictly to the poetry itself, and a few major critical documents. Much of what is to be said has often been said before; but most of the short general treatments of the field were written some time ago. There has been much detailed work and many shifts of taste in recent years. I have tried to take account of these, and, without any particular search for novelty, to write from the point of view of contemporary critical opinion.

Part of this book was written while I was Visiting Lecturer at Johns Hopkins University, Baltimore: I should like to thank my colleagues there for a year's work in a delightful environment. I am also grateful to Professor Basil Willey for his helpful criticism.

CHAPTER I

GRAY

THE word 'romantic' has so many meanings, and they are so ill distinguished from each other that one is sometimes tempted to feel that it is hardly worth using it at all.[1] However, in practice it is difficult to get along without it, and we may begin by using it in its least ambiguous sense, as it is used in the title of this book, as a mere chronological label, to describe the imaginative literature of the early part of the last century. It is not hard to see where the label ought to be tied: in fact a new conception of poetry does come into being towards the end of the eighteenth century, and the poets who were to work it out were all either dead or past their creative period by 1825. In fact, too, the label is more than chronological; it does more than point to a certain group of writers; it can also legitimately connote something about their work, some things that they really had in common in spite of very different life-histories and personal characters. In the first place, the major poetry of this period is all written under the influence of the new secular, liberal conception of man and his destiny that had sprung from the French Revolution and the French eighteenth-century thought that had preceded it. I avoid saying inspired by the French Revolution, for that would suggest that the poetry is predominantly political and social, which it is not: and it would fail to suggest what is certainly true, that a reaction against the revolutionary ideal is almost as important as the revolutionary ideal itself. Secondly, the scepticism about existing society engendered by the revolutionary ferment impels the more imaginative minds into a new communion with nature. When the world of man is harsh and repugnant, in need of violent reform, yet so often, it appears, irreformable, the poet is apt to seek consolation in the world of nature which does not need reforming: at first *natura naturata*, the lovely texture of the

7

visible world; then *natura naturans*, the informing principle within it:

> A motion and a spirit that impels
> All thinking things, all objects of all thought,
> And rolls through all things—

whose dwelling is as much in the mind of man as in "all that we behold of this green earth". The proper study of mankind is still indeed man, as it was in the eighteenth century, but man seen less often in relation to his fellows or to a fixed religious scheme, and more often in relation to the natural universe of which he is a part.

Often it seemed that this communion with nature had been more fully achieved in ages past than in modern society. "The world is too much with us", Wordsworth complains in 1806. "Little we see in Nature that is ours": he would rather be a "Pagan suckled in a creed outworn" than live the commonplace modern life, cut off by cares of the world from the deeper sources of joy. More often it is not to classical paganism that the poets now turned; from that, after all, the standard cultural tradition was derived. They found greater freshness and naturalness in little-known or barbarous ages which post-Renaissance culture had neglected. They turned to the medieval past, often indeed with ignorance of its real nature, but finding in it various kinds of liberation which we shall later have to discuss; especially perhaps liberation from the conscious ego that education, convention and society had built up. For the motive behind all these excursions into nature and the middle ages is a new subjectivism. When Pope, in the heart of the Augustan age, sets out to write a great philosophical poem he writes an *Essay on Man*, on man in general. When Wordsworth, at the beginning of the next age, wishes to do so he starts by writing *The Growth of a Poet's Mind*—meaning the growth of his own mind, his own personal development. The emphasis shifts from social man to the individual man, when he is alone with his own heart or alone with nature. Those who feel that man is most himself in society will probably get their greatest poetical satisfaction from the poetry of other ages. Those who feel that man is most himself in solitude (or at most, perhaps, in a solitude made for two) will naturally turn to the poetry of the romantic age.

These, then, are the themes we shall be discussing in the following pages, and their origins all go far back into the eighteenth century. But one must begin somewhere, and since, in a book of this size, it is more profitable to talk about poets and poems than about movements and trends, we will try to illustrate the relation between the poetry of the new age and that of the eighteenth century by the case of the poet Gray, whose difficulties and triumphs throw much light, by contrast or anticipation, on what the later romantic poets were trying to do.

Gray's production is so scanty and so much of it is in a very minor mode, that one may well wonder why he seems to occupy such a key position in the history of English poetry. True, he happened to write one of the greatest poems in the language; but he only did it once, and it is hard to believe, if it were not for the *Elegy*, that we should be very interested in the rest of his poetry, except in a spirit of historical curiosity. His letters are of far greater volume, and are delightful as examples of that kind of friendly yet elegant and well-mannered correspondence which seems now to have passed from our culture. They are not strenuous writing; the historian of ideas will not find much of his material in them; but the historian of sentiment, of ways of feeling, will find a great deal. However, if we really want to discover what Gray's work amounts to, we should read the poems and the letters together, for they do much to illuminate each other. The picture of Gray that emerges from his letters is not a very vigorous or happy one. He was charming, generous of his time and trouble, devoted to his friends as they were to him, but he suffered from a constitutional melancholy.

Mine, you are to know, is a white Melancholy, or rather Leucocholy for the most part; which, though it seldom laughs or dances, nor ever amounts to what one calls Joy or

Pleasure, yet is a good easy sort of a state, and *ça ne laisse que de s'amuser*. The only fault of it is insipidity; which is apt now and then to give a sort of Ennui, which makes one form certain little wishes, that signify nothing. But there is another sort, black indeed, which I have now and then felt . . . it believes, nay, is sure of everything that is unlikely, so it be but frightful; and on the other hand, excludes and shuts its eyes to the most possible hopes and everything that is pleasurable; from this the Lord deliver us! for none but he and sunshiny weather can do it.[2]

Many of his literary projects were abortive, and were undertaken in a spirit almost of resigned hopelessness.

I am a sort of spider; and have little else to do but spin my web over again, or creep to some other place and spin there. Alas! for one who has nothing to do but amuse himself, I believe my amusements are as little amusing as most folks. But no matter; it makes the hours pass, and is better than [to pass one's life in ignorance and grossness].[3]

Indeed, if we desert literary history and look at Gray in terms of common life, how could he have been happy? He lived the life of a timid and reclusive don, the major peripeteia of his existence being to cross the road from Peterhouse to Pembroke in 1756: and he achieved few of the successes that make such a course worth while. One of the most learned men of his day, he left behind hardly any result of his scholarship; when ultimately elected to the Regius Professorship of Modern History, he could never bring himself to lecture; interested in society, he could see the great world only by proxy, through his friendship with the brilliant Horace Walpole; and when he engaged in literary discussion, his most serious interest, it was commonly with his inferiors, with Mason, for instance, a worthy and devoted, but after all somewhat asinine person. Poor Gray, a sensitive poetical misfit in the hearty and idle grossness of eighteenth-century Cambridge, with little emotional

experience to express in verse except the sense of being a
misfit, of being a failure as a specimen of social man.

This sense of maladjustment is not uncommon among the
poets of the later eighteenth century. Gray's melancholia, the
madness of Collins, Smart and Cowper—it is possible that they
had a more than personal cause. All these men were trying to be
poets in a climate of feeling that did not suit what ought to have
been their kind of poetry.[4] They were acutely aware of conflict
and unrest within themselves; yet the poetic dialect of their
time offered no means of expressing it—the language for doing
so was not yet invented. A generation or so later all was to be
changed. When Shelley feels as Gray must often have felt, the
result is *Stanzas Written in Dejection*. But the strong social sense
of eighteenth-century poetry, its very good manners made this
kind of self-expression quite impossible. There was as yet no
convention for communicating one's private griefs to the world.
In some ways this was for the best; perhaps the romantic age
was to produce too many stanzas written in dejection, and too
easily. No doubt the experience of doing it was highly thera-
peutic to the poet. To Gray no such direct relief was possible,
and we turn to his early poems somewhat puzzled to find what
he was really writing about. The *Ode on the Spring* is on the face
of it a conventional piece of poetizing; we can see very little of
the spring because the Hours, the Zephyrs, Contemplation and
the Muse insist on standing in the light. Where we meet a
particularly felicitous phrase we find it duly acknowledged in
the footnotes as an adaptation from Shakespeare, Virgil,
Milton or Matthew Green. (This kind of quotation is a legitim-
ate and acknowledged source of eighteenth-century poetic
imagery, unknown to the romantic age, but revived in our own
day by Mr. Eliot.) We are invited to sit with the Muse and
think

> How vain the ardour of the Crowd,
> How low, how little are the Proud,
> How indigent the Great!

—though why we should think so in the spring more than at
any other season is not apparent. The most vividly realized

aspect of the spring is, somewhat oddly, its insect life. And then we discover that this is because

> To Contemplation's sober eye
> Such is the race of Man:

—as ephemeral as the insects and as busy about nothing. However, Contemplation is not allowed to have the last word: the insects answer back:

> Methinks I hear in accents low
> The sportive kind reply:
> Poor moralist! and what art thou?
> A solitary fly!
> Thy joys no glittering female meets,
> No hive hast thou of hoarded sweets,
> No painted plumage to display:
> On hasty wings thy youth is flown;
> Thy sun is set, thy spring is gone—
> We frolick, while 'tis May.

And here, surely, is what the poem is really about, what Gray really wants to do—to contrast the free and fluent energy of spring with his own solitary and constricted life, so deficient in the sources of joy. And this is the only way he can do it: only after four stanzas of conventional description and conventional moralizing can he even begin to say what he wants, and then only under the guise of a rather rococo joke. We find the same side-step into facetiousness in the letters whenever the approach of a real emotional intimacy seems imminent. The *Ode on a Distant Prospect of Eton College* is a much more considerable performance. Gray had been happy at Eton; all the high spirits and most of the tenderness he was ever to know were encountered there: but even in this poem the sense felt so acutely by Gray of a happiness enjoyed in childhood, inevitably to be lost in later life, appears less as an experience than as a piece of traditional Stoical-Christian moralizing. And the same could be said of the fine *Hymn to Adversity*.

The greatness of the *Elegy in a Country Churchyard* no one has ever doubted, but many have been hard put to it to explain in what its greatness consists. It is easy to point out that its thought is commonplace, that its diction and imagery are correct, noble but unoriginal, and to wonder where the immediately recognizable greatness has slipped in. "That triumph of an exquisitely adjusted tone", I. A. Richards has called it; and that is certainly part of the truth. The poem is written with the most perfect of good manners. The reader is not hectored or dazzled, the commonplaces are presented to him as what they are, and he is made to feel that on such a theme they are far more in place than any attempt at novelty. But surely this is not all. Rare and agreeable as perfect manners are, they do not make a great poem any more than a great man. If we read the *Elegy* in the light of the letters and the Odes cited above, we may see more clearly what Gray was about. In the earlier poems he had been struggling with the difficulty of expressing personal conflicts and despondencies within the limits of eighteenth-century poetic convention. He had not succeeded very far. In the *Elegy* he finds the answer to his problem, finds the complete expression of his private despairs and frustrations, yet the whole perfectly and unobtrusively placed in a wider field of reference. The *Elegy* was most probably begun soon after the death of Gray's school friend West, some reminiscences of whom remain in the conclusion of the poem. West had been Gray's dearest friend and confidant, and like himself a melancholy and hypochondriac young man. The "youth to fortune and to fame unknown" of the closing epitaph might be either West or Gray himself, and is, indeed, by a process familiar to dream-analysts, a sort of fusion of the two. Dr. Tillyard has cogently argued that *Lycidas* derives its emotional force from Milton's identification of Henry King with himself.[5] Something of the same kind seems to be going on in the *Elegy*: and the Gray-West persona, the obscure young man who dies with his ambitions unfulfilled, is further assimilated to the rude forefathers of the hamlet, the village Hampdens and Miltons who have suffered the same fate. So Gray is enabled to sum up the experience of all his years of adult life—the melancholy, the obscurity, the lack of vigour and achievement, and yet see it in a way that makes it tolerable—as part of the inevitable human situation.

The poem begins with what looks like a drawing from nature: it is actually full of literary echoes. The bell tolling for the dying day comes from Dante; that unelegiac creature the beetle had already been consecrated to poetic purposes by Shakespeare and Collins, and the owl seems to be behaving in an extremely self-conscious manner. Gray is here far less concerned with nature as an object of contemplation than with his readers—the readers whom he wishes to lull into a resigned, acquiescent, summer-evening frame of mind. The opening picture is followed by some extremely obvious reflections about the sights which the rude forefathers of the hamlet will see no more. They are designedly obvious—again intended to establish the mood of calm acquiescence in which the poem must be read. We then come to what Gray really wants to say.

> Let not Ambition mock their useful toil,
> Their homely joys, and destiny obscure;
> Nor Grandeur hear with a disdainful smile,
> The short and simple annals of the poor.
>
> The boast of heraldry, the pomp of pow'r,
> And all that beauty, all that wealth e'er gave,
> Awaits alike th'inevitable hour.
> The paths of glory lead but to the grave.
>
> Nor you, ye Proud, impute to these the fault,
> If Mem'ry o'er their Tomb no Trophies raise,
> Where thro' the long-drawn isle and fretted vault
> The pealing anthem swells the note of praise.

The proud (Horace Walpole *et hoc genus omne?*) come out as badly as in the *Ode to the Spring*, and their arrogance is pointless, since their end will be the same as everybody else's. The lines that follow, on the rustic Hampdens and Miltons whose narrow lot has prevented their developing their capabilities, are often read mechanically because so many of them have become familiar quotations. They deserve closer attention. Gray is saying in the first place that in society as we know it many such cases must occur; further, he is saying that this is a part of the order of nature, and therefore must occur in any conceivable society.

> Full many a gem of purest ray serene,
> The dark unfathomed caves of ocean bear:
> Full many a flower is born to blush unseen,
> And waste its sweetness on the desert air.

And this is not a matter for unmitigated regret. A flower presumably prefers not to be picked, as Mr. Empson has remarked,[6] and a gem can hardly be supposed to care whether it stays at the bottom of the sea or not. We think that this is waste, but that is only because we take a false and partial view: obscurity may be a positive advantage. The narrow lot of the villagers circumscribed not only potential virtues, but potential crimes—forbade them the brutality of a conqueror or the venality of a court poet. It is noticeable that the literary vices—

> The struggling pangs of conscious truth to hide,
> To quench the blushes of ingenuous shame,
> Or heap the shrine of Luxury and Pride
> With incense kindled at the Muse's flame

—get considerably more space than the political ones, and one begins to suspect that Gray is actually far more concerned with the frustrated poet than the frustrated ruler. And from here we can realize what is going on beneath the surface of the poem. The obscurity that is being discussed is Gray's obscurity. The consolation offered for waste and frustration in the human situation generally is *a fortiori*, a consolation to Gray's own sense of waste and frustration, which no longer appears as a personal inadequacy, but as a part of what must inevitably happen in all human life and all nature. Gray is enabled to bear his own disappointments by seeing them in the wider setting of

which they are a part. The personal reference becomes more
evident in the closing lines. The listless youth, muttering his
wayward fancies in solitude and dying young, is in the first
place West, who, like Milton's Lycidas, cherished poetic
ambitions that were frustrated by an early death. Secondly, he
is Gray himself, West's *alter ego*, also ambitious, hypochondri-
acal and unhappy, and likely enough to come to a similar end.
The Epitaph sums up the whole, and provides another argument, and to Gray the final one, for the attitude of resignation
which he wishes to establish.

> No farther seek his merits to disclose,
> Or draw his frailties from their dread abode,
> (There they alike in trembling hope repose,)
> The bosom of his Father and his God.

After all this talk about success and failure, ambition and
frustration, we realize that we have been talking in purely
human terms, and they can never be enough. We do not, after
all, know what success or failure is, the final judgement must
rest with God, who alone can remedy human and natural
injustice, and complete its insufficiencies.

We need no longer ask where the noble commonplaces of
the *Elegy* derive their compelling force. They are compelling
because they are not only what they first appear, majestic
statements about the common lot: they are also the solution of
Gray's personal problem, and perhaps the only one possible in
his day. Not a contented member of his own society, "no
longer at ease in the old dispensation", Gray, nevertheless,
lived too early to see any likelihood of a new one, in which
human capacity, his own included, could be more fully employed. His only possible solution, therefore, is a kind of
elegiac Toryism—since it is inevitable that some flowers must
remain unpicked, and some gems lie unregarded about the
bottom of the ocean, we must all resign ourselves to this
possibility and realize that in any case the final solution to these
perplexities is outside the realm of human estimation altogether.
And further, since both human dignity and poetic decorum—
the whole convention of communication at the time—forbid

one to complain individually about this, the only way to express this complex of emotions and reflections is to generalize it, to get rid of one's personal conflicts by absorbing them in a greater whole.

To the coming romantic age both the problem and the solution were to appear very differently. When, in the first rumblings of the revolution, the whole fabric of society was changing before one's eyes, there was no need for resignation.

> Bliss was it in that dawn to be alive
> But to be young was very heaven.

The revolutionary generation were willing enough to admit that society today is full of waste and frustration, but tomorrow this is all to be remedied—on earth. If we wish to realize to ourselves the spirit of the revolutionary part of the *Prelude*, or of *Prometheus Unbound*, we must understand the spirit of the static, unchanging society that had preceded them. It is too easy to accept the romantic liberals at their own valuation—as the unacknowledged legislators of the world to come: and too easy to write them off in terms of modern political reaction—the reaction of crisis and disillusionment—as adolescent enthusiasts. Gray had perfectly good historical reasons for writing as he did; and was besides saying something that is permanently true. The romantic liberals in the next generation had equally good historical reasons for writing as they did, and were expressing a hope that is also a perpetually recurrent part of human experience.

The Romantics, besides, were not to be faced with Gray's difficulties in personal expression. After the lessons of Rousseau had been learnt it was no longer necessary to feel that private emotion and intimate experience must be excluded from direct literary expression. The barriers to communication are cast down, emotion pours itself forth unrestrained and undisguised; it had no longer to be submitted to the elaborate process of absorption and transmutation to which Gray subjected it. Gray writes

> To each his sufferings: all are men,
> Condemned alike to groan.

While Shelley can write

> I could lie down like a tired child,
> And weep away this life of care:

—often with some loss of the dignity given by reticence, but with a corresponding gain of immediacy. The poet has become not a reflective literary person speaking to other reflective literary persons, but a man speaking to men.

The two other poems of Gray that bulk largely in literary histories, *The Progress of Poesy* and *The Bard*, have quite a different interest. They are more purely literary in inspiration, and have little reference to experiences other than literary ones. As his correspondence shows, Gray was deeply interested in questions of poetic technique and diction; though, since his correspondents were not very exacting, he did not pursue them as strenuously as one would have liked. His general position is indicated in an early letter to West.

> "As to matter of stile, I have this to say: The language of the age is never the language of poetry; except among the French, whose verse, where the thought or image does not support it, differs in nothing from prose. Our poetry, on the contrary, has a language peculiar to itself; to which almost everyone that has written, has added something by enriching it with foreign idioms and derivatives. Nay sometimes words of their own composition and invention. . . . In truth, Shakespear's language is one of his principal beauties; . . . every word is in him a picture."[7]

Gray then appears as the supporter of a special poetic diction, different from the ordinary language of the time, and Wordsworth rightly singles him out as his special opponent when he comes forward with his own theories of poetic diction in the next age. What Gray is saying here is not typical of the eighteenth century as a whole. In fact, a great deal of earlier eighteenth-century poetry—most of Pope, for instance—is written in an adaptation of the cultivated speech of the day. It

is Pope's special distinction to have raised this kind of speech
to its highest potential, and nothing more brilliant in this way
is ever likely to be seen than the portraits in the *Prologue to the
Satires*, Clarissa's speech in *The Rape of the Lock*, or the
Gotterdämmerung at the close of the *Dunciad*. But Gray and
his friends were on another track. They were in pursuit of what
Gray called "the true lyric style, with all its flights of fancy,
heightenings and inversions". They were thus rather conscious
amateurs of enthusiasm and wildness: Mason wrote some very
enthusiastic odes in which the wildness was conscientiously put
in, as from a pepper-pot, after the first draft. Gray is aware,
within the limitations of friendship, of Mason's worst absur-
dities. But it is to be feared that he himself accepts and reinforces the notion that poetical qualities can be pinned on to
prose ideas, rather as though one were trimming a hat. He
writes to Mason, of a passage in one of his poems:

> "It is flat, it is prose. . . . If the sentiment must stand,
> twirl it a little into an apophthegm, stick a flower in it, gild it
> with a costly expression, let it strike the fancy, the ear, or
> the heart, and I am satisfied."[8]

Few people, I think, would maintain this attitude today,
and it is against it that the campaign inaugurated by Wordsworth in *Lyrical Ballads* was especially directed—with considerable justification, as we feel when we turn to the *Progress of
Poesy* and *The Bard*. Indeed, these two accomplished but
unfortunate pieces have been under fire from both sides, for
Johnson attacks their 'cumbrous splendour' in one of his most
annihilating pieces of criticism.

Of what do these cumbrous splendours consist? Generally
speaking, in a steady avoidance of the normal way of putting
anything. "Gray thought his language the more poetical the
more remote it was from common use," Johnson justly remarks.
The Progress of Poesy is heavily incrusted with mythological
ornament: all abstractions—the Cares, the Passions, the Sports
and the Pleasures are resolutely personified, while concrete
things are as likely as not turned into abstractions—the corn-
fields, for example, become 'Ceres' golden reign'. Gray is at

pains to turn everything he wants to say into imagery, generally
visual imagery, but as often as not he has to explain in footnotes
what the images are intended to convey. This we might forgive
if they really stood on their own feet, were really effective for
their own sake: but for the most part they remain vague and
unrealized.

> With arms sublime, that float upon the air.
> In gliding state she wins her easy way:
> O'er her warm cheek and rising bosom move
> The bloom of young Desire, and purple light of Love

Venus' arms are not sublime because they were a particularly magnificent pair, but merely because they are uplifted;
and her cheeks and bosom are not intermittently exposed to a
mauve spotlight, but merely fresh-coloured.* This trick of
using words in a Latin sense different from the common one
is an exaggeration of a habit of Milton's, and if we look into it
we discover that a great deal of the diction of this kind of poetry
is a not very successful adaptation of Milton's habits of style.
Venus winning her way 'in gliding state' may be compared to
Milton's fruit that 'hung amiable' from the boughs. Both are
phrases that are effective in a purely verbal way, and do not
give any clear sensuous or even intellectual impression. In
Milton there is every reason for writing like this: he is faced
with the problem of describing superhuman personages,
uncorrupted or unearthly landscapes, and he rightly chooses
a style of generalized grandeur, without any too vivid sensuous
realization. When this is done by lesser poets on lesser occasions
the effect is of vague pastiche, sculpture in marble imitated in
stucco. Similarly the clustering of mythological, historical and
geographical names has, in Milton, a functional justification.
He is writing the history of mankind, on the largest scale, and
all that men have done or thought, in Damasco, Marocco or
Trebizond, beyond the Mexique bay or on the plains of
Sericana, is relevant to his scheme, is even necessary to people
his vast empty distances. But when Gray uses the same device

---

*Sublimis—raised on high; purpureus—brightly coloured.

in his own small-scale poem, and with none of the Miltonic
impulse, the result suggests rather mechanically applied
ornament: and when, in the second antistrophe of the *Progress
of Poesy*, he resolutely takes the Muse on an expedition to cheer
up the Eskimos, stopping (on the way home, I suppose) to hear
the savage youth repeat their lessons in Chili's boundless
forests—well, we can only assume that Gray is not really thinking, or at least that he is only thinking of writing something
that looks like poetry. And, indeed, that is the trouble with this
kind of work, it is too like poetry: not poetry, but too like it.

A similar barren self-consciousness is seen in his treatment
of metaphor. Johnson complains that in the first strophe Gray
has confounded the images of spreading sound and running
water. So he has, but quite deliberately: he is evidently proud
of it and adds a footnote to tell us what he has done and what it
all means. "The subject and simile," he says, "as usual with
Pindar, are united." He means to suggest that we have here one
of the metaphors in which, under the pressure of a powerful
imaginative impulse, two contrary ideas are fused together
into a single image. In fact, we have nothing of the kind; the
imaginative pressure is not there; the music and the water
remain separate, and we are left in a state of slightly uneasy
confusion as to which is being talked about. Gray and Mason
were great connoisseurs of all the outward signs of emotion in
poetry, but unhappily they thought that these could legitimately be used without the underlying emotion. They
conscientiously cultivated "wildness", aposiopesis, broken and
extravagant utterance: "Here it is the brokenness, the un-
grammaticalness, the total subversion of the period that
charms me", wrote Gray to Mason of a passage in one of his
poems: as if these things had any value in themselves. Con-
sequently they were apt to choose 'wild' and extravagant
subjects, and for this purpose they thought it best to frequent
remote ages and little-known civilizations.

Gray was a student of Welsh and Norse literature, and
Mason was an ardent but uncritical Celticist. Gray was a real
scholar, and indeed could not approach any subject except
through the medium of a cultivated scholarship. But his

motive in adopting Norse and Welsh themes, in *The Bard*, *The Fatal Sisters*, *The Triumphs of Owen* and *The Descent of Odin*, was not mainly scholarly: he appears to think that by writing of those barbarous cultures in which the passions might be supposed to be both stronger in themselves and less inhibited in expression, the want of passion in his poetry, perhaps also in his life, might be supplied. *The Bard*, the sister ode to *The Progress of Poesy*, is the best example of this. What we have said of the style of *The Progress of Poesy* applies equally to *The Bard*: but we find it in even more strongly the attempt to flog into life, by purely stylistic devices, a passion that is not really there. The theme, the supposed denunciation, by the last of the Welsh bards, of Edward the First, the English invader, fulfils all Gray's requirements: it is medieval, Celtic, therefore "wild"; it requires powerful and violent feeling and therefore by Gray's canons, extravagance of expression, and it affords the opportunity for a historical pageant in the prophecy of the fate of Edward's line. Gray could not write without competence and distinction: but alas, all is there except the one thing needful. Let us anticipate a little, and quote Wordsworth's criticism of this kind of poetry, written perhaps with Gray's ode in mind.

"The earliest poets of all nations generally wrote from passion excited by real events; they wrote naturally and as men: feeling powerfully as they did, their language was daring and figurative. In succeeding times, Poets and Men ambitious of the fame of poets, perceiving the influence of such language, and desirous of producing the same effect without being animated by the same passion, set themselves to a mechanical adoption of these figures of speech . . . sometimes with propriety, but much more frequently applied them to feelings and thoughts with which they had no natural connection whatsoever. A language was thus insensibly produced, differing materially from the real language of men in any situation."[9]

Why then trouble with these poems, if they are merely

littérature, in the contemptuous sense in which Verlaine used the word? Mainly because they are an early symptom of discontent with the Augustan orthodoxy, an early attempt to establish a freer and wider use of poetic language. Although an abortive and mistaken attempt they remain historically important, especially as they provide in a sense the starting point for the Wordsworthian revolution. It is a sonnet of Gray's which was to provide Wordsworth with a text to illustrate the pseudo-poetic diction against which his own verse was a protest.

It would be ungrateful to leave Gray on this carping note. His consciousness of unfulfilment, of the need for a new flowering of the sensibility was not made up or affected, but wholly genuine. A calm disillusionment with society and with worldly success finds its supreme expression in the *Elegy*. But one cannot live in the mood of the *Elegy* at all times, not even if one is a naturally elegiac soul like Gray; and later in life he begins to find the fulfilment he desires in a new relation to the world of nature. He made journeys to the Lake district and to other parts of England and Scotland, at first, perhaps, as a deliberate amateur of the picturesque, like many others of his day. But he found something more than the picturesque—a beauty untroubled by passion or desire, which could speak directly to his own heart, a communion more satisfying, perhaps, than any he had known with human beings.

In the evening walk'd alone down to the Lake by the side of Crow-Park after sunset and saw the solemn colouring of night draw on, the last gleam of sunshine fading away on the hill-tops, the deep serene of the waters, and the long shadows of the mountains thrown across them, till they nearly touched the hithermost shore. At distance heard the murmur of many waterfalls not audible in the day-time. Wish'd for the Moon, but she was *dark to me and silent, hid in her vacant interlunar cave.*[10]

In passages such as these, Gray finds the way out of the impasse into which his life seems to have led itself, and we see

him as an earlier and less adventurous explorer of the path that
Wordsworth was to follow.

NOTES

CHAPTER 1. GRAY

1. v. A. O. Lovejoy, *The Discrimination of Romanticisms*. Publications of
the Modern Language Association of America, 1924; and R. Wellek *In
Defence of the Term Romanticism*. Comparative Literature, 1949.

2. *Gray's Correspondence*, ed. Toynbee and Whibley, I, 209.

3. ibid. I, 194.

4. The point is made by Mr. F. L. Lucas in *The Decline and Fall of the
Romantic Ideal* (1936).

5. E. M. W. Tillyard, *Milton*, pp. 80-5.

6. In *Some Variations of Pastoral*, p. 4.

7. *Correspondence*, I, 192.

8. ibid. II, 568.

9. Appendix on Poetic Diction (1802) to Preface to *Lyrical Ballads*.

10. *Correspondence*, III, 1089.

CHAPTER II

WORDSWORTH AND COLERIDGE

i. The Young Wordsworth

THE scientific and philosophical revolution of the seventeenth century bore its fruit in the eighteenth. Its most obvious result was a general sense of reassuring certainty, a sense that many dark corners had been thoroughly swept and illuminated by clear daylight. Newton had laid bare the nature of the physical world, Locke that of the human mind, and henceforth, though there might be many details to fill in, it was felt that the general scheme of things was pretty well understood. Understood in much the same way as the working of a machine could be understood; Newton's physics was essentially mechanistic in outlook, and later writers such as Hartley developed from Locke's premises a mechanistic psychology to match. In philosophical and even in religious discussion mechanical imagery was common. A favourite simile for the universe was "this great machine", and Pope observed with gratification that a machine which worked so satisfactorily could not be without a plan. This mechanistic tendency was not necessarily irreligious—where there was a plan there must be a planner, and writers like Paley who endeavoured to prove the existence of God from the evidence of the visible creation commonly began with the simile of a watch. If you found one lying on the ground you might not understand its purpose, but you would certainly, as you came to examine it, be obliged to acknowledge in it the evidences of conscious design; and from there you would be led inevitably to the hypothesis of a designer. So it was with the natural world. The more you studied it the more exquisitely it appeared to be contrived, and the more certainly you were led to a reverence and admiration for its Contriver. This type of argument, and the evidence on which, in the eighteenth century, it was based, is seen at its clearest in Paley's celebrated *Natural Theology*, an admirably written work, of cheerful and commonsense piety, which afforded the utmost satisfaction to many solid believers, and certainly did nobody any harm. It is, however, possible to object that it affords very little satisfaction to man's deeper religious apprehensions. If Nature is an excellently contrived machine, then God becomes an extremely skilful Mechanic; and indeed, as has often been remarked, there is little in the rationalistic theology of the eighteenth century to suggest that God is other than the great Engineer who originally designed the machine, set it in motion, and then left it to run by itself. This is in fact the Deist position; and though Theism and Revelation held their own, Deism is probably the central religious movement of the age.[1]

Locke's general philosophical attitude, the cool dry light of his intellect, his preference for clear and distinct ideas, led also to a sharpening of the distinction between what was believed as truth and what was merely enjoyed as fiction. In a writer like Sir Thomas Browne it is commonly hard to be sure in which realm we are moving; mythology and science not only rub shoulders, but often, it appears, enter into some illicit congress. After the beginning of the eighteenth century this is no longer possible; it becomes increasingly necessary to distinguish fancy from philosophy and fable from fact. This becomes clearly evident in poetry and the criticism of poetry. The whole symbolical machinery of earlier poets is now only available as an avowed fiction or an agreeable toy. The business of the sylphs in *The Rape of the Lock* is satisfactory and successful because nobody was in any sense asked to believe it. Johnson dislikes mythology and the pastoral convention, and condemns *Lycidas* on that ground. "Its form is that of a pastoral, easy, vulgar and therefore disgusting. . . . Where there is leisure for fiction there is little grief." And we have seen the difficulties Gray got into in trying to write poetry other than that of reasonable reflection.

The fact is that the concept of Nature, which seemed at first to offer a liberation from so many barbarous and obscurantist errors, had become by the end of the century a prison-house for the emotions. Nature meant human nature, which the eighteenth century already knew all about, since the Ancients had described it rightly by instinct, and the modern philosophers had further illuminated it by science. It also meant the visible frame of things, whose workings were becoming steadily more familiar. Yet as the universe became ever more well paved and brightly lit there seemed to be less and less on which the emotions could fix themselves with satisfaction. The great machine aroused after all only a temperate reverence, and its Architect a rather distant respect. Those who felt an instinctive need for a stronger and more intimate response to experience were often driven to seek it in fiction, failing to find it in the great world. This is the ultimate motive behind much exploration of mediaeval, Norse and Celtic tradition, behind such literary deceptions as Chatterton's poems and Macpherson's Ossian. Yet they were unsatisfactory because they were after all no more than fiction, and some of them plain forgery.

Those born wholly within this well-cultivated garden could hardly expect to find their way out of it; their feet had grown too accustomed to the gravelled footpaths. The experience of the few solitary eccentrics, like Blake, who lived on the shaggy heath outside was too peculiar to be generally accessible to their fellows. The real poetical revolution could only be accomplished by one whose birth and education was within the eighteenth-century cultural pattern, yet on the edge of it, within sight of other kinds of experience. This was Wordsworth's position. Born at Cockermouth, and early removed to school at Hawkshead on Esthwaite, he grew up on the fringe of a wilder, less tidily economic country than most of rural Britain, and in a society materially and spiritually different from the normal English squirearchy. The "statesmen" of the Westmorland and Cumberland valleys were a race of independent yeomen, the last survivors of an English peasantry, something very different from the tenant-farmers or the landless cap-touching labourers which was all that the enclosures had left in most parts of England. Independence and equality were the keynotes of this society; in his boyhood experience Wordsworth, as he

tells us, had hardly met the notion of a social superior. The
early experience of a social hierarchy no doubt predisposes the
mind to the notion of a hierarchy of accepted ideas. In his
remote upland valleys Wordsworth knew neither. All good
North-countrymen know that the south (which begins at about
Derby) is decadent and feebly conformist. Wordsworth had his
share of this feeling, and it helped to create the sturdy in-
dividuality without which he could never have transformed the
face of English poetry.

On the other hand, at Cambridge a little and more in
France, Wordsworth came fully into contact with the most
vigorous intellectual life of his day. He inherited the eighteenth-
century cultural tradition and received the full impact of contemporary philosophic and political movements. The combined
influences of solitude and society, of nature and the converse
of men, in forming his mind are described in *The Prelude*, that
incomparable poetic autobiography, which is a better source of
information on Wordsworth's life than anything that has been
written about him by others. More than that, and besides being
one of the greatest reflective poems in the language it gives us
a strongly drawn contemporary picture of the impact of the
Revolution on the young sensibilities of the age.

The Prelude was to have been the introduction to *The
Recluse*, a vast philosophical work, of which *The Excursion* forms
the first part, and of which otherwise only a fragment under
the original title survives. It is to be suspected that the most
vital parts of what Wordsworth had to say were said in *The
Prelude*, and that that is why the design was never completed.
It is perhaps best read in the earliest version, that of 1805, for
Wordsworth continued to revise it throughout his life; and
although the alterations were often improvements, he also,
alas, often falsified his own early ideas and impressions to suit
the cautious conservatism of his later years. It is no accident
that the most beautiful and most spontaneous passages in *The
Prelude* occur chiefly in the first two books, 'Childhood and
Schooltime', for the impressions of his early years formed the
deepest and most significant layer of Wordsworth's later thought.
The picture of a childhood on the shores of Windermere and

Esthwaite is an idyllic one, and it would be idle to paraphrase what has been said perfectly once and for all. The central idea of this part of the poem is to show the powerful and necessary bond between nature and the human mind. But nature is no longer the great machine of the eighteenth century; it is a being with a soul and purpose of its own, linked inevitably with the human soul and its purposes. Wordsworth is not writing as a philosopher—he does not set out to explain this relationship, and we do not know whether he sees the soul of the world and the soul of man as separate substances, yet akin and capable of communication, or whether he really holds a kind of pantheism—that the soul of man is a temporarily separated fragment of the totality of being, to which in the end it will return. This pantheist view seems to be suggested by *A Slumber did my spirit seal*, the last of the Lucy poems, and we find traces of it in *Tintern Abbey* and elsewhere. Later, Wordsworth tended to disguise it in the interests of Christian orthodoxy, but it always remained, perhaps, the real groundwork of his religion.

The most memorable passages in the early books of *The Prelude* are not analytical: they are incomparable descriptions of incidents in his childhood where it seemed that he actually felt in Nature a moral and spiritual presence, moulding and working on his mind as a human teacher might have done, though more mysteriously and profoundly. Alone, for instance, on the hills at night, engaged in trapping birds, he fell to the boyish temptation of taking a bird from another's snare. But the invisible monitor is watchful over even this venial fault, and as soon as the deed was done

> I heard among the solitary hills
> Low breathings coming after me, and sounds
> Of undistinguishable motion, steps
> Almost as silent as the turf they trod.
> (I. 329)[2]

Though Wordsworth insists constantly, both here and elsewhere, on the moral influence of Nature, the dominant

impression is not of being watched over by a censorious mentor ,
but of communion with a vast invisible presence, felt perhaps
at the most unlikely times, when climbing rocks after birds'
nests, for instance, an object which he admits to be a mean
one: yet the danger of the slippery crags and the closeness of
his contact with them brings a half-physical, half-spiritual
sense of communion with something beyond the visible frame
of things.

> Oh at that time
> When on the perilous ridge I hung alone
> With what strange utterance did the loud dry wind
> Blow through my ears The sky seemed not a sky
> Of earth, and with what motion moved the clouds.
>
> (I. 346)

Rowing on the lake one night, he observed before him a
huge peak which suddenly appeared to him as an animated
presence, 'as if with voluntary power instinct' and seemed to
stride after him 'with measured motion, like a living thing':

> and after I had seen
> That spectacle, for many days, my brain
> Worked with a dim and undetermined sense
> Of unknown modes of being; in my thoughts
> There was a darkness, call it solitude,
> Or blank desertion, no familiar shapes
> Of homely objects, images of trees,
> Of sea or sky, no colours of green fields;
> But huge and mighty Forms that do not live
> Like living men, mov'd slowly through the mind
> By day and were a trouble to my dreams.
>
> (I. 417)

The occasion itself is trivial: yet what is being described is
evidently close to mystical experience: and it is such experience
that is at the source of Wordsworth's most living work. Wordsworth, too, is being led to God by the contemplation of Nature:
but by a different route from Paley's Natural Theology.

It is a temptation to linger among these early scenes, to dwell particularly on the incomparable descriptions of simple animal joys, of skating, fishing, exploring the islands on Windermere. But if we did there would be no end to quotation. It is noticeable that there is little mention of intellectual influences; when in a later section he writes ostensibly of books the only ones actually mentioned are *Don Quixote* and *The Arabian Nights*. He goes out of his way to depreciate scientific thought; addressing Coleridge, the friend for whom the *Prelude* was written, he says with satisfaction

> to thee
> Science appears but what in truth she is,
> Not as our glory and our absolute boast,
> But as a succedaneum, and a prop
> To our infirmity.   (II. 216)

The third book, on residence at Cambridge, has a pious interest for Cambridge men, but is plainly written with a lower degree of intensity than what precedes it. Wordsworth's most vivid experiences did not come to him in his undergraduate days, which appear mostly as an interlude of careless and cheerful companionship and some uncertainty of purpose—

> And more than all, a strangeness in my mind,
> A feeling that I was not for that hour,
> Nor for that place.   (III. 80)

In those spacious and unregenerate days the demands of a formal syllabus were not exacting, and if mediocrity was given little stimulus to screw itself up a few painful inches higher, genius was left to its own devices. Wordsworth studied English and Italian poetry, and showed some aptitude though little love for mathematics. It is noticeable that whenever the springs of Wordsworth's emotional life temporarily fail he can fall back on a perfectly competent logical intellect. For all the apparent aimlessness of his youth, there was a strong element of hard northern common sense in Wordsworth: and though he was

never one of those who mainly approached the world through
the channels of a formal education, he made himself perfectly
capable of using the goods of the mind for his own purpose.
What that purpose was became clear to him in his first long
vacation, when in a walk on the mountains, returning home
after a cheerful party, he realized as dawn broke that he was
going to be a poet.

A holiday journey to France and Switzerland in 1790
provided the material for *Descriptive Sketches*, written in
couplets in the manner of the eighteenth-century topographical
poets, and written well enough, but without much sign of
Wordsworth's individual power. More important than the
scenery, however, was the political atmosphere; and it is from
now onwards that political and public events begin to play a
major part in Wordsworth's development. The air of Cambridge is commonly sympathetic to other people's revolutions,
and Wordsworth and his fellow-traveller Jones were already
prepared to be excited by what was going on across the Channel.
The new-born Revolution was at its phase of sublime hopeful-
ness, when all things seemed possible

> France standing on the top of golden hours,
> And human nature seeming born again.
>   (VI. 353)

They actually landed in Calais on the eve of the day when
the king was to swear fidelity to the new constitution, and the
whole nation was mad with joy. Abstract political feeling was
not yet much in Wordsworth's line, but the scenes they
actually witnessed on this journey gave his mind a bias from
which it was afterwards only turned away at the cost of half
his poetic life. A short and indeterminate return to London
was followed by another visit to France at the end of 1791.
After his childhood in the Lakes this was the most formative
period of his career. At this time Wordsworth lived more
intensely than he was ever to do again.

His first sympathies with the Revolution were mainly
sentimental, and he was actually far more engrossed by the

daily novelty of life and manners. He settled first at Blois,
then at Orleans, moving first in the kind of respectable society
where the turmoil of the times was not mentioned, and himself
remaining ignorant of what was really going on. Becoming
bored with this company, he began to mix with the common
world, which was better suited to his natural cast of mind.
Born in a district where manners had a homely natural equality,
he had never felt the claims of wealth and blood as anything
very real, and the social ethics of the early revolution excited
him less than they might,

> Seemed nothing out of nature's certain course,
> A gift that rather was come late than soon.
>
> (IX. 253)

Thus without any formal adoption of a creed, by natural
sympathy, Wordsworth became what was then called a Patriot,
and felt the people's cause as his. He was confirmed in his
position by a solitary Patriot among his early friends, one
Beaupuy, the only one among the otherwise royalist officers
Wordsworth had first consorted with to support the popular
cause. He has his honourable place in Book IX of *The Prelude*,
but even from these lines it would probably be easy to under-
estimate his effect on Wordsworth's mind. Beaupuy was
evidently a man of great maturity and force of character. A
combined impression of nobility and charm emerges from the
passages in *The Prelude* where he is described; also the sense
that the young Wordsworth, perhaps for the only time in his
life, indulged the generous sentiment of hero-worship. A rather
stuffy arrogance is undoubtedly the defect of the later Wordsworth; but at this stage love, friendship, admiration, intellectual
and moral excitement combined to make the current of his life
flow more freely than it had done since his boyhood. If in
Cambridge he had been out of his due place and time, here in
France he felt himself at the centre of things. Through Beaupuy
he felt himself vicariously a patriot and a man of action, and he
contrasts his phase of abstract political discussion 'in academic
groves' with the sense of participation in a great historical

process that his present situation gave him. Many men who were of Wordsworth's age in the 1930s had similar experiences in Spain, and some carried their engagement in the struggle much farther. But nothing in modern literature communicates the experience with the fullness and nobility of these books of *The Prelude*.

Wordsworth and Beaupuy were Jacobins by temperament, and were not among those desiccated sectarian progressives in whom political passion destroys the sense of the past. Walks in the neighbouring forest and along the castled banks of the Loire aroused memories of days gone by, partly historic, partly fanciful.

> Imagination, potent to enflame
> At times with virtuous wrath and noble scorn,
> Did also often mitigate the force
> Of civic prejudice, the bigotry
> So call it, of a youthful Patriot's mind,
> And on these spots with many gleams I looked
> Of chivalrous delight.   (IX. 495)

Yet this coincided with the steady formation, under Beaupuy's direction, of liberal and republican principles, and a clear view of what the essentials of the political struggle were. When the two friends met one day a wretched peasant girl, languid with hunger, Beaupuy exclaimed in agitation," 'Tis against *that* that we are fighting": and both believed that within a little time misery of that kind would have vanished from the earth.

At the same time something else was happening, of crucial importance in Wordsworth's emotional life, which *The Prelude* nevertheless does not record. Wordsworth fell in love with a French girl, Annette Vallon, had a daughter by her, but parted from her on his eventual return to England in 1792. The affair was not clandestine in the obvious sense: Wordsworth's sister Dorothy was in his confidence, both of them corresponded with Annette after his return to England, and went to visit her in Calais on the eve of his marriage. Later,

Wordsworth's wife and her family also seem to have known of the facts. But no direct reference to it appears in his writings. Which of the various circumstances that commonly prevent young Englishmen from making their attachments abroad more permanent was active in Wordsworth's case we cannot say. An impulse of strictly limited candour led him to incorporate a disguised and greatly modified version of the story as an interpolated tale in the first version of *The Prelude*. This was later taken out and printed separately as *Vaudracour and Julia*. The feebleness of the poem, poetically and morally, does not necessarily show that he had any grave sense of personal embarrassment in the matter, but it does seem to show that he was trying to cut this experience out of his poetic career. Nevertheless, the political excitement of the French part of *The Prelude* is obviously accompanied by an emotional excitement for which we may suspect a more than political cause. Mr. Herbert Read has argued that Wordsworth's really creative period is simply the afterglow of this one patch of intense emotional experience. I think this is overstated, but if we ask for the reasons for Wordsworth's 'fifty years' decay', one of the answers will certainly be this deliberate cutting himself off from the emotional springs of his young manhood.

What does appear, clearly analysed as well as powerfully communicated, in *The Prelude*, is the progress of Wordsworth's political sympathies. Details of time, place and circumstance are confused, and neither need we trace them any more minutely. His close contact with the revolution at work began in October 1792, when he moved to Paris. It was two months after the deposition of the king, and a month after the September massacres, the thought of which gave him a foretaste of the horrors to come. Paris was for the moment quiet,

> But at the best it seemed a place of fear,
> Unfit for the repose which night requires,
> Defenceless as a wood where tigers roam.
> (X. 80)

Then followed the conflict between the Jacobins and the Girondins; and Wordsworth suffered the distress of seeing the growth of the tyrannical Jacobin power at the expense of the Gironde which to him stood for the ideals of human and rational liberty with which the Revolution had started. He was deeply troubled, and for a time considered abandoning his status as an Englishman, identifying the cause of France with that of humanity, and throwing in his lot with the Girondins. To what extent he did so is not quite clear; at any rate the connexion did not last long; and compelled probably by a mixture of motives (though in *The Prelude* he reduces them to one—lack of money) he returned to England at the end of 1792.

The confused and powerful impressions of his stay in France had all been received, but they had not yet been digested. A period of real mental stress, even of torment, began on his return to England. In February 1793 England joined the allies and declared war on the French republic. This was the first violent shock ever received by Wordsworth's moral nature. The Revolution had been to him almost a thing of course, in tune, as it seemed, with the nature of things and the bent of his own mind. Even its premonitory terrors had been what the less intense and immediate kinds of fear often are, something of a stimulus. Now he was exposed to a violent conflict of loyalties. He encountered the real agony (the extremities of this position are little known to Englishmen, and better known to the twentieth century than to Wordsworth's day) of having to abandon either loyalty to his own country or his deepest intellectual and moral convictions. He describes the confused misery of sitting in church, where a village congregation to which by all local and natural sympathies he is bound, are praying for English victories; and he alone is unable to join in.

Before any solution to this impasse, the Terror started in France. Wordsworth describes it in one of the most powerful passages of *The Prelude*, and describes too the desolating effect it had on all who had placed their ideal hopes in the Revolution. We know more about how revolution works in these days, and have been forced to blunt our minds to horrors. Wordsworth writes, without self-dramatization, in a passage of simple veracity, that for months and years after the end of the atrocities

I scarcely knew one night of quiet sleep,
Such ghastly visions had I of despair
And tyranny, and implements of death,
And long orations which in dreams I pleaded
Before unjust tribunals, with a voice
Labouring, a brain confounded, and a sense
Of treachery and desertion in the place
The holiest that I know of, my own soul.

(X. 374)

The horrors were ended by the execution of Robespierre in 1794. Wordsworth's hopes, hopes in the people rather than in their leaders, took on a new lease of life, countered only by the bitter scorn and indignation against the English political leaders who insisted on fighting what seemed the inevitable course of nature and justice. The whole of this development is summarized in a retrospective passage in Book X of the *Prelude* (74 *et seq.*). But from the time that 'with open war, Britain opposed the liberties of France' a change began to take place, not only in Wordsworth's opinions but in his whole attitude to the world. The gradual transformation of revolutionary France, through the exigencies of war, into an oppressive and conquering power was a further shock to his susceptibilities. Until this time the current of his feelings had run undisturbed, and his development had been mainly a natural development of feeling. Now that his emotional unity was torn apart he was obliged to fall back on the rationalizing intellect. At first he felt a sense of pride and triumph

To look through all the frailties of the world,
And, with a resolute mastery shaking off
The accidents of nature, time and place,
That make up the weak being of the past,
Build social freedom on its only base,
The freedom of the individual mind,
Which, to the blind restraints of general laws
Superior, magisterially adopts
One guide, the light of circumstances, flashed
Upon an independent intellect.   (X. 820)

The mentor whom he chose to guide him along this difficult path was probably William Godwin, the chief of a group of writers whose main historical function was to translate the principles of French revolutionary thought into English. But Godwin was also a far from negligible independent thinker, admirable for the integrity of his system, and for the consistency with which he pushed philosophic anarchism to its last conclusions.

The passage quoted above is a fair description of his doctrine as it appears in *Political Justice* (1793). His powerful influence on the liberal opinion of his day, notably on Wordsworth and Shelley, is well known; but *Political Justice* is a book more talked about than read. We shall have to return to it in speaking of Shelley, and it has been admirably summarized elsewhere,[3] so I will not spare space to analyse it here. It is easy, however, to see its attraction for a young intellectual. Its unbounded confidence in reason, its clear and rigid argument, might well seem to provide a sure foothold for one like Wordsworth whose original emotional faith had been shaken.

For a time the sense of being cut loose from painful emotional ties was a liberation; Godwin's uncomprising spirit corresponded to a sternness in Wordsworth's own nature; as he says,

> I took the knife in hand,
> And stopping not at parts less sensitive,
> Endeavoured with my best of skill to probe
> The living body of society
> Even to the heart.
>
> (X. 874)

However, Godwin is violently unhistorical, he is completely without the natural piety that is the foundation of Wordsworth's being, his only emotion is a sombre exaltation at the ultimately inevitable triumph of his principles. Wordsworth was not formed by nature for this kind of mental activity, yet not daring to trust to the emotions that had been so harshly betrayed, he continued grimly the attempt to base a faith on abstract reasoning.

> Thus I fared,
> Dragging all passions, notions, shapes of faith,
> Like culprits to the bar, suspiciously
> Calling the mind to establish in plain day
> Her titles and her honours, now believing,
> Now disbelieving, endlessly perplexed   (X. 889)

The result might have been foreseen. Wordsworth had been through a period of great moral and emotional strain. He had come, as it seemed, to an impasse, and was trying to get out of it by a method for which, indeed, he had plenty of intellectual toughness, but for which temperamentally he was quite unsuited. He continued to work against the grain

> till, demanding proof,
> And seeking it in everything, I lost
> All feeling of conviction, and, in fine,
> Sick, wearied out with contrarieties,
> Yielded up moral questions in despair.
>   (X. 897)

It was a moral crisis about whose details we have very little information, even its exact date and duration remaining obscure. What is clear is that it marked the end of a road for Wordsworth. The revolutionary fervour and the doctrines of the age of reason had played their part in forming his mind, but they could carry him little further. It is in the nature of things that revolution can never be a permanent ideal, and any attempt to make it so transforms it into something else. Wordsworth was beginning to learn by bitter experience what has become a commonplace to our generation. Having received his dusty answer he seemed for a time to have nothing to look forward to: but, after how long an interval we do not exactly know, it became apparent that new life and new hope were flowing in upon him from entirely different sources.

The agents of Wordsworth's regeneration were his sister
Dorothy, and Coleridge. After his return to England he spent
a time in uncertain wanderings; then, in 1795, he established
himself first in Dorset, then in Somerset with Dorothy, who had
been his childhood companion and at all times a devoted friend
and confidante. Late in that year the first meeting with Coleridge took place, and so began the enchanted period when the
'three persons with one soul' walked, talked and lived together,
in one of those rare associations that combine exhilaration and
serenity. The effect of this new-found happiness on Wordsworth was gradual. It was perhaps two years before the Godwinian ice was entirely melted out of his heart; the feeling of
the period is of a grateful and blessed return to what he now
recognizes to be his own proper path. Dorothy not only loved
Wordsworth perhaps more deeply than anyone else ever did;
she was also the exquisitely receptive sharer of all his deepest
joys. Dorothy was a direct link with his childhood, and her
presence carried him back both to the homely earth-bound
affections and the mystical exaltations of that time. In a
lovely passage of the *Prelude* he tells how her influence

> like a brook
> That did but cross a lonely road, and now
> Seen, heard and felt, and caught at every turn,
> Companion never lost through many a league,
> Maintain'd for me a saving intercourse
> With my true self.   (X. 911)

The influence of Coleridge is less easy to define. It was in
the first place intellectual, and showed Wordsworth another
road to travel than the Godwinian one. The enormous reading
of Coleridge's studious youth had given him a mind far more
richly stored, of far greater range and variety than Wordsworth's. His bent was towards philosophy of an idealist and
speculative kind, infinitely richer in poetic suggestion than the
rationalism of the revolutionary thinkers. Coleridge's soaring
fancies were anchored by Wordsworth's deep-rooted alliance
with nature and common experience. So began the most fruitful
association in the history of English poetry.

ii. The Great Decade

The Wordsworths first came to visit Coleridge at Nether Stowey in 1797, and charmed with the neighbourhood and the company, found a house for themselves at Alfoxden near by. From then began the series of walks and talks out of which grew the idea of Lyrical Ballads. It is hard to reproduce the state of mental excitement that gave rise to this revolutionary collaboration. Much of it must have been in Coleridge's talk, and no surviving document has been able to do justice to that. It may seem that Wordsworth had had enough mental excitement in his recent period of storm and stress: what came now, however, was excitement of the steadier and slower-burning kind, involving the whole of a man's nature, from which creative work is most likely to arise. Up to now Wordsworth had written little really good poetry:[4] since we must, I think, describe *The Borderers* as a failure, and *Descriptive Sketches* and *Guilt and Sorrow* as abortive attempts to deliver the essential Wordsworthian truth. Coleridge provided a torrent of new and exciting ideas, some of them concerned with poetry and criticism, but some of them going far beyond this; for he was already beginning to develop what was ultimately to be his chief message to the nineteenth century—that no way of thinking could be adequate that did not involve the whole of a man's nature, his moral and metaphysical as well as his empirical experience. Wordsworth, on the other hand, a slower and more silent partner, contributed a far greater weight and depth of moral experience. He had been swept away on a turbulent flood and was now beginning to feel his feet on the ground—a sensation which remained unknown to Coleridge throughout his life. In all that we read of the origin of *Lyrical Ballads* this spiritual division of labour is apparent. During the first year of their association, as Coleridge tells us,

> "—our conversation turned frequently on the two cardinal points of poetry, the power of exciting the sympathy of the reader by a faithful adherence to the truth of nature, and the power of giving the interest of novelty by the modifying colours of imagination.

In this idea originated the plan of *Lyrical Ballads*: in which it was agreed that my endeavours should be directed to persons and characters supernatural, or at least romantic; yet so as to transfer from our inward nature a human interest and a semblance of truth sufficient to procure for these shadows of imagination that willing suspension of disbelief for the moment that constitutes poetic faith. Mr. Wordsworth, on the other hand, was to propose to himself as his object to give the charm of novelty to the things of every day, and to excite a feeling analogous to the supernatural by awakening the mind's attention from the lethargy of custom, and directing it to the loveliness and the wonder of the world before us."[5]

This is the classic passage in Coleridge's *Biographia Literaria* that announces the opening of two new roads in English poetry. Coleridge's psychological and philosophical interests are sufficiently prominent both here and in Wordsworth's preface to the second edition of *Lyrical Ballads*. For Wordsworth tells us that the aim was "above all, to make these incidents and situations interesting by tracing in them, truly though not ostentatiously the primary laws of our nature: chiefly as far as regards the manner in which we associate ideas in a state of excitement." Experiments were to be made in using, not the conventional diction of poetry, but "the real language of men" (we shall discuss the implications of that phrase in the next section); and the subjects were to be taken from humble and rustic life, because in such circumstances the essential passions of the heart developed more freely and fully, and were enriched by mingling with "the beautiful and permanent forms of nature"—this last item being clearly Wordsworth's contribution to the declaration of faith. When we turn to the volume itself we find at first little sign of these theoretical preoccupations, but it is not out of place to mention them briefly in advance, for there is no doubt that a good deal of theorizing of this kind preceded the actual composition of the poems.

A word or two on the bibliography of this period will be helpful. The first edition of *Lyrical Ballads* appeared in 1798, anonymously. Coleridge's contribution was *The Ancient Mariner*, the most considerable poem of the collection, and three minor fragments—*The Foster-Mother's Tale*, *The Nightingale* and *The Dungeon*. A second edition appeared in 1800, under Wordsworth's name alone, with one additional poem by Coleridge—*Love*, and a large number by Wordsworth. This edition also contains the first form of Wordsworth's famous preface expounding his poetic faith. A third edition of 1802 greatly expands the preface and adds an appendix on Poetic Diction; the fourth edition of 1805 has only textual changes. *The Prelude* was probably begun in 1799, and was complete in the first version by 1805. And in 1807 Wordsworth published *Poems in Two Volumes*, consisting entirely of new work, including the *Immortality Ode*, *Memorials of a tour in Scotland* and many of the best sonnets. It was in this decade, from 1797-1807 that nearly all his best work was done. Coleridge's *Christabel* was intended for inclusion in *Lyrical Ballads*, but was not finished in time, and did not in the end appear till 1816.

The aspect of *Lyrical Ballads* that presented the most obvious challenge to the general poetry-reading habits of the age was the choice of modest and familiar themes, subjects drawn from "humble and rustic life" expressed in "the real language of men". It was on Wordsworth's part quite a conscious challenge and suffers at times from the defects of all such conscious challenges. The whole question of the proper material of poetry is a difficult one; one might put it crudely by saying that any subject is possible if you can get away with it. Themes such as *The Idiot Boy* and *Goody Blake and Harry Gill* had not formerly been celebrated in English poetry: the question of whether they should have been is a vexed one, since there are no categorical imperatives in the arts. Coleridge, whose criticism of *Lyrical Ballads* we shall shortly discuss, probably said the last effective word when he doubted whether the emotional tension in such pieces was sufficiently great to justify their being written in verse. One cannot help feeling that

Wordsworth sometimes followed a doctrinaire opinion about humble and rustic life rather than his own real poetic impulse —in *Goody Blake*, or *Simon Lee*, for instance. In *The Idiot Boy* a real imaginative intuition about the strangeness and incommunicability of the poor crazy child's moonlight adventures seems to be struggling in a waste of garrulity and trivial expression. In *The Thorn* triviality of expression is deliberately assumed as a dramatic device, but as Coleridge pointed out, gives way to a sudden magnificence in the seventh stanza—a magnificence which is out of character, yet almost manages to cast its pervasive radiance over the whole poem. It is when he is least anecdotal, when he relies most on a straight unanalysed impression, that Wordsworth succeeds best in conveying the pathetic simplicities that have moved him. The fragment *Animal Tranquillity and Decay*, for instance, is a small nugget of Wordsworth which one might very well use as a sample to show the essential quality of the whole.

In the greatest of the rustic poems no such questions arise. They are mostly found in the second edition of *Lyrical Ballads* in 1800, and include *Michael* and *The Brothers*. *Michael* is described as a pastoral poem; and it is indeed a poem about shepherds; but the label seems puzzling if we think of earlier senses of "pastoral"; for though Dr. Johnson might quite likely have found *Michael* "easy, vulgar and therefore disgusting", it would certainly have been so in a very different sense from *Lycidas*. It is completely without the conscious literary artifice that we associate with pastoral poetry, and free from the trick of using rural simplicities to light up some sophisticated situation. But it has the essential quality of pastoral—the imaginative sympathy for a life of unselfconscious simplicity from which the poet, merely by being a poet, is detached.

> It was the first
> Of those domestic tales that spake to me
> Of shepherds, dwellers in the valleys, men
> Whom I already loved; not verily
> For their own sakes, but for the fields and hills
> Where was their occupation and abode.

And hence the tale had a special importance in Wordsworth's life, for it marks the stage when he was led on from the
pure passion for nature to feel for passions that were not his
own

                                    and think
        (At random and imperfectly indeed)
        On man, the heart of man, and human life.

Arnold wrote of Wordsworth that his greatest strength
was in his power of making us feel "the simple primary human
affections and duties"; and it is noticeable that the poems of
rural life generally deal with the simplest and most primary of
all—the bond between parents and children. Wordsworth
rarely writes much about love between man and woman, and
when he does it is often broken and unhappy. The figure of
the forsaken mother often occurs in his poetry—perhaps
because of the misadventure in his own biography. In *Michael*
the theme is love of a father for his son: it is told in blank verse
of a rather stiff simplicity, and much of it is straight narrative
so unelaborated that it treads on the verge of the prosaic. But
the grave movement of the blank verse avoids the sudden
slippery descents of some of the stanza poems. Equally it avoids
the interspersed, detachable splendours and beauties that we
find elsewhere, the obviously lovely lines and stanzas that
stand out from passages of less intensity and make an immediate effect. The effect of *Michael* is not immediate: more
prolonged acquaintance with the poem reveals it as that most
characteristic Wordsworthian achievement—a poem where a
long familiar emotion, that has been absorbed into the personality and is no longer clamorous or importunate, is evenly
diffused throughout. Its sublime or moving passages do not
call attention to themselves and might easily pass unnoticed—
for example, the famous line describing how the old man,
broken down by the absence and the failure of his son, went
out to work on the sheepfold they had begun together, but had
not the heart to add to it

        And never lifted up a single stone.

Many of these poems, however, can hardly be said to describe affections and passions: they are records of chance encounters, unimportant in themselves, yet transfigured by some sudden moment of illumination. *The Leech Gatherer* is one of these, and the core of the poem is in the stanzas (XVI–XIX) in which the old man ceases to be an individual old man and becomes a vague archetypal figure, symbolical of—what? Wordsworth says Resolution and Independence, and tags on a neat moral to give the poem a clear significance. As often, however, the neat moral is an afterthought and is soon forgotten, since Wordsworth was easily misled about the source of his inspiration, and the heart of the experience was not an ethical intuition that can be explained, but a mystical one that can hardly be explained at all, only presented. Readers of Wordsworth must learn to expect a good deal of material and circumstantial detail in his poetical experiences: it is sometimes obstructive, but it is also what gives us the sense that he has his feet on the ground far more firmly than any other poet of his age. When the experience is less cluttered up with circumstance and explanation it can find expression in flashes of that magical and immediate loveliness in which Wordsworth is sometimes supposed to be deficient. This is so in *The Solitary Reaper*, where there is no narrative thread and no moral—just a girl singing as she reaps a field:

> A voice so thrilling ne'er was heard
> In spring-time from the Cuckoo-bird
> Breaking the silence of the seas,
> Among the farthest Hebrides.
>
> Will no one tell me what she sings?
> Perhaps the plaintive numbers flow
> For old, unhappy, far-off things,
> And battles long ago:

—lines which catch the *lacrimae rerum* more memorably than those of any poet since Virgil.

The five Lucy poems were written in Germany in 1799 and

appeared in the third edition of *Lyrical Ballads*. The most probable suggestion about their origin is that they represent a transmutation of Wordsworth's feeling for his sister Dorothy. No poems illustrate more clearly than the first three Wordsworth's power of conveying emotion by the simplest and most reticent means. And the last two are brief and pregnant expressions of two of the foundations of Wordsworth's thought —*Three years she grew* of the influence of Nature on the formation of human life, and the epitaph, *A slumber did my spirit steal* of his austere pantheism.

> No motion has she now, no force,
> She neither hears nor sees,
> Rolled round in earth's diurnal course
> With rocks, and stones, and trees.

Theories about the language of common life do not prevent Wordsworth using the rich and unusual word 'diurnal', which seems to cast a glow over the almost monosyllabic simplicity of the rest of the poem.

As we have seen, one of the objects of *Lyrical Ballads* was a psychological one—not merely to describe interesting or pathetic incidents, but to use them to illustrate what Wordsworth rather grandly calls "the primary laws of our nature", and the way in which we "associate ideas" in the presence of emotion. This last phrase is a relic from the philosophical doctrine held strongly by Wordsworth and Coleridge at this time—the associationism of Hartley. Hartley was an estimable but now outmoded writer, who had developed, basically from the thought of Locke, an elaborate system of psychology, deriving all human emotions, passions and thoughts from the mechanical association of sense impressions. These sense impressions are received passively by the mind, and character and mental life are built up entirely from them. Hartley's great influence at the close of the eighteenth century is hard to understand today, but he is worth mentioning here, for though both Wordsworth and Coleridge progressed to other philosophies of life later on, associationism left an abiding mark on Wordsworth's

thought. It is Hartley's contention that since our minds
are built up entirely by "association", it is extremely important
to make the right impressions and associations in early life.
This provides the philosophical background for Wordsworth's
belief in the influence of natural objects in the formation of
character, and perhaps too goes far to account for his sturdy
reliance on immediate sensuous experience, his abstention from
the fanciful and arbitrary, his feeling that his verse must "deal
boldly with substantial things". Which does not mean important or impressive things. Many of the puzzlingly trivial poems
in *Lyrical Ballads* were significant to Wordsworth for precisely
these psychological reasons. The child in *We are Seven* has not
yet experienced death as a fact, it is merely a word to her, so
she still feels that she is one of seven brothers and sisters. The
child in the *Anecdote for Fathers* is pressed to give an intelligible reason for preferring one place to another, long before he
has formed any such reasons, and when he is conscious only of a
confused sense of well-being; so he is eventually driven to take
refuge in fabrication. And as the sub-title of the poem suggests,
this innocent fabrication can lead easily to lying. These are,
perhaps, interesting case-histories, but not very successful
poems. In the first of the Lucy poems, however, the beautiful
Strange fits of passion have I known, the motive is the same. The
sudden dropping of the moon behind the cottage roof brings
into the lover's mind, by an association that is at once natural
and lovely, the fear that his Lucy may too have disappeared
from mortal eyes.

This reliance on the immediate experience, the belief that
this, rather than any intellectualizing power, is the agent of
education and the father of poetry, is explicitly stated in what
are, perhaps, the two key poems of *Lyrical Ballads*, from the
doctrinal point of view—*Expostulation and Reply* and *The
Tables Turned*. In the first the poet is reproached by a friend for
sitting idly on a stone dreaming his time away. He replies in
lines which sum up the Wordsworthian version of Hartley's
doctrine, and illustrate, too, the state of contemplative calm
that Wordsworth had come to rely on after the storm and stress
of the Revolution and Godwinian intellectualism.

The eye, it cannot choose but see;
We cannot bid the ear be still;
Our bodies feel, where'er they be,
Against or with our will.

Nor less I deem that there are powers
Which of themselves our minds impress;
That we can feed this mind of ours
In a wise passiveness.

In *The Tables Turned* the poet retorts upon his friend, exhorts him to leave his books and come out into the open, since he can learn more about man and about moral good and evil from the spring woods than from all the sages. We might object that an impulse from a vernal wood cannot in fact teach us anything at all about good and evil, and that Wordsworth is only getting back from Nature the moral values that he himself has put in. Science and the philosophies derived from it have accustomed us to thinking of Nature as morally neutral, and indifferent to the desires and purposes of man. However, the lines that follow are more easily acceptable.

Sweet is the lore which Nature brings;
Our meddling intellect
Misshapes the beauteous forms of things:
We murder to dissect.

Beneath a half-playful and even superficial opposition to science and philosophizing, there is the wholly serious demand, central to Wordsworth's faith, for a total response by man's nature to the non-human nature around him. Those who are worried by Wordsworth's habit of finding sermons in stones are free to give up that side of his work, but they would also be wise to remember the remark of a later poet, Yeats, extremely unlike Wordsworth, that in the poet's church there is an altar but no pulpit; and that morals drawn from the lesser celandine are not the core of Wordsworth's belief. Another poem, the *Lines Written a Few Miles above Tintern Abbey*, is needed to supplement those just discussed.

In *Tintern Abbey* it is at once apparent that we have a poem written in an altogether higher style. The air of familiar anecdote is abandoned, and the embarrassing playfulness that sometimes appears in Wordsworth's domestic pieces totally disappears. Reading *Tintern Abbey* in conjunction with the slighter pieces in *Lyrical Ballads* we feel that they are the data on which this great reflective poem is based, that the intellect has been used, not for meddling or dissecting, but to fuse into a whole the scattered impressions for which commonly 'in consequence of the film of familiarity and selfish solicitude we have eyes, yet see not, ears that hear not, and hearts that neither feel nor understand'. The occasion of the poem is a visit to the Wye, already visited five years before: this gives rise to reflections on the significance that the landscape has had for him in the interval. Wordsworth first restates his moral doctrine: the memory of this beautiful scene has been not only calming and restorative, but has aroused almost unnoticed sensations of pleasure, which have had their results in impulses of kindness and love. This seems truer and more adequate than saying that a wood in spring can teach you all about ethics. But he has also owed to these recollections another and sublimer gift:

> —that blessed mood,
> In which the burthen of the mystery,
> In which the heavy and the weary weight
> Of all this unintelligible world,
> Is lightened:—that serene and blessed mood,
> In which the affections gently lead us on,
> Until, the breath of this corporeal frame
> And even the motion of our human blood
> Almost suspended, we are laid asleep
> In body, and become a living soul.

Wordsworth does not explain or defend this doctrine; he merely states it as experience, in verse of such serene loveliness that it carries with it its own guarantee of authenticity. This is the part of the Wordsworthian religion that no change in the intellectual concept of nature is likely to invalidate, and that

pace Mr. Aldous Huxley,[7] can be as active in tropical jungles
as in the dales of Westmorland. However, Wordsworth does
not stop here: he goes on to trace the stages through which his
response to nature has passed. First the "glad animal movements", the mainly muscular pleasures of his boyhood; then,
in youth, the purely visual delight in natural beauty,

> That had no need of a remoter charm,
> By thought supplied, nor any interest
> Unborrowed from the eye:

—then in maturity the development of a sense, which is only
the full realization of something obscurely experienced all
along—

>   —a sense sublime
> Of something far more deeply interfused,
> Whose dwelling is the light of setting suns
> And the round ocean and the living air,
> And the blue sky, and in the mind of man;
> A motion and a spirit that impels
> All thinking things, all objects of all thought,
> And rolls through all things.

This is a profound and undoctrinal pantheism, unfettered
by moral accretions at a more superficial level. Wordsworth felt
obliged to play it down in later life, in the interests of orthodoxy; and others have felt bound to abandon it in the face of
the scientific 'neutralization of nature'. But it remained after all
the most deeply based of all Wordsworth's experiences; it is
after all wholly independent of any particular belief about the
nature of the physical world, even of any particular culture;
and it is likely, therefore, to remain an important part of
modern religious experience.

In *Tintern Abbey* Wordsworth is far more willing than his
theories would suggest to use the full resources of the English
vocabulary. In the more exalted passages of this, as of most of
the reflective blank-verse poems, the influence of Milton is
apparent. A little later this becomes more obvious and we

sometimes find Wordsworth using a Latinized and abstract vocabulary, commonly supposed to be most uncharacteristic of his work, and directly due to Miltonic influence. We can see it in *Yew-Trees*:

> Huge trunks! and each particular trunk a growth
> Of intertwisted fibres serpentine,
> Upcoiling and inveterately convolved;
> Nor uninformed with Phantasy, and looks
> That threaten the profane.

So much for the language of humble and rustic life.

In 1802–3 Wordsworth's political interests revived, as we can see from the sonnets of that year, which was important to him both for its public and its private events. In 1802 he married Mary Hutchinson and, before the wedding, paid another brief visit to France, apparently for the purpose of seeing his daughter and making a final settlement with Annette. The sonnet on Westminster Bridge was composed on the way, and his meeting with his child is recorded in *It is a beauteous evening, calm and free*. These are followed by a series of political sonnets which form a new and important development of Wordsworth's work. In this year, the Peace of Amiens was concluded with France, and this was on the whole welcomed by liberal sympathizers; but disillusionment was soon to follow. It became evident, as, sooner or later, in most revolutions it becomes evident, that what had begun as a movement of liberation was ending in a personal despotism. In August 1802 Napoleon was made consul for life, and to the upholders of the early Revolutionary ideal, this was a betrayal. Wordsworth attacks it, from the standpoint of the old guard of liberal idealists; the other sonnets written at Calais in this year record his sense of shame and scorn for what was going on. In the course of the same year, the new Italian republics and the German states became obviously mere satellites of the Napoleonic power; a French army suppressed an attempted revolt in Switzerland; and an attempt by France to recover San Domingo was resisted by the negro patriot Toussaint L'Ouverture whose heroism and misfortunes aroused much liberal sympathy throughout Europe. No doubt there are other views of these events than those held by Wordsworth, who saw them in terms of simple black and white—liberty and serfdom; not having the benefit of the Marxist-Hegelian dialectic which would have taught him to subsume them both in the higher synthesis of a universal dirty grey.

In 1803 the war broke out again, and this time an attack on England was expected; so to the motives of disillusioned political idealism were added those of alarm and straightforward patriotism in the face of a national danger. All these phases of opinion are reflected in Wordsworth's sonnets of 1802–3, and are combined too with an apprehension about the stagnant worldliness that he felt in the England of that time. These poems mark the end of another period in Wordsworth's biography. After this time it was hardly possible for an Englishman to preserve the pristine faith in the revolutionary mission of France. It is customary to reproach Wordsworth with abandoning it, which is absurd; even Romantic poets must be permitted to grow up. What we can legitimately regret is that he abandoned so much with it, so many of the ideals that should have been immune to historical disappointment. The word liberty becomes gradually emptied of its former content, and is identified with English national security: a proper object of solicitude indeed: but it must be confessed that the exhortation to

> Save this honoured Land from every Lord
> But British reason and the British sword

falls somewhat tamely on the ear after the ardours of *The Prelude.*

The effect of this second injection of political feeling on Wordsworth's poetry is debatable. Conventionally, his sonnets on public affairs are numbered among the great ones of the language. Gerard Manley Hopkins once complained that there was too much white neckcloth about them—meaning too much sententious moralizing; a view with which I cannot help agreeing. If we compare them with the French parts of *The Prelude* we feel that Wordsworth is now simply telling us about his political opinions, not re-creating his political passions. His model was Milton rather than the earlier Renaissance sonnet-eers. Milton had tended to depersonalize the sonnet, to substitute a kind of abstract dignity for the sensitiveness to all the complexities of feeling that had been the glory of the earlier sonnet-writers. It is possible that the effort was a mistaken one, that a poem as short and as formally complex as the sonnet needs complexity and delicacy of feeling to correspond, unless it is to become empty. But Milton has always a secure and unshakable sense of style. This Wordsworth has not. When he is writing from the more superficial layers of his mind he is capable of horrid flatnesses which he apparently does not notice. (These are particularly damaging in the sonnet, which is too small to be able to afford waste matter.) Hence, after the panegyric on Venice in which the imagination has been really touched, the wretched dilution of the closing lines—

> Yet shall some tribute of regret be paid
> When her long life has reached its final day.

Hence the vague and somewhat fusty exhortations of the *Men of Kent* sonnet, and even, if I may dare to say so, of *Milton thou should'st be living at this hour*. The Calais sonnets are free from this, and it is tempting to suggest that it is because they were touched with the power of the ancient flame: the visit to Calais was a link with the ardour of his youth: the sonnets composed on his return were part of the process of settling down. But great sonnets of the personal and reflective kind are found throughout Wordsworth's work—among the finest being *Surprised by Joy, impatient as the wind*, written in 1815; and the exquisite *Mutability*, from the late and mostly dismal series of *Ecclesiastical Sonnets*.

The sonnets mark the development of a more conscious, more literary manner which was to grow on Wordsworth in later years, though he was always to use it somewhat uncertainly. But when the emotional springs are deeply tapped he now becomes as capable of deliberate grandeur as any poet in the language—as we can see in the *Ode on the Intimations of Immortality*. Like so much of the best of Wordsworth, it is a piece of spiritual autobiography, composed between 1803 and 1806. That is to say, it was partly contemporary with the *Prelude*, of which its substance might have formed a part. But it is composed with far more literary artifice, in long strophes with varied line-lengths of the kind that were supposed, in remote imitation of Pindar, to be peculiarly suitable for odes. Wordsworth handles this difficult scheme magnificently, and the poem has a sustained lyric splendour of which we have hardly any other example in his works. It is also notable because it is built on a piece of poetic faith that is something less than whole-hearted, nearer to Coleridge's "willing suspension of disbelief" than is usual with Wordsworth. The theme is the gradual decline in keenness of imagination as we pass from childhood to maturity.[6] Wordsworth connects it with a sort of Platonic belief in pre-existence, a belief that

> Our birth is but a sleep and a forgetting,
> The soul that rises with us, our life's star,
>   Hath had elsewhere its setting
>   And cometh from afar.

And this is certainly something that Wordsworth did not hold as an article of faith. But if he is here presenting his subject, as he rarely does, in an almost mythological guise, he has lost none of his power of dealing plainly with the facts of experience. The development described is as true to the movements of his own heart as the least elaborated passages of the *Prelude*, and beneath the quasi-Platonic myth is the essential truth that the deepest springs of his inspiration are in his childhood.

But we must not go too far with Wordsworth before returning to Coleridge's poetry of this time. *The Ancient Mariner* was, equally with Wordsworth's contribution to *Lyrical Ballads*, a product of their life together in Somerset. It was begun on an excursion in 1797, originally as a joint venture.

Wordsworth contributed a line or two, and the idea of the crime for which the Mariner was to be punished. But the poem soon became Coleridge's alone. Indeed, his imagination worked in a very different way from Wordsworth's—which was why they could stimulate each other, but also why it would have been almost impossible for them actually to collaborate. Coleridge, on his rare creative occasions, had the power to do what Wordsworth rarely attempts—to embody his conceptions in a myth: but that is putting it wrongly, for the myth precedes the conceptions. Wordsworth's best poetry is reflective, Coleridge's is symbolical. "It is not possible," Yeats wrote at the end of the century, "to separate an emotion or spiritual state from the image that calls it up and gives it expression." In Wordsworth it often is possible: in Wordsworth's greatest poetry, in *Tintern Abbey*, for example, images are being found for emotions and spiritual states that preceded them. In *The Ancient Mariner* the images come first, and express something more, or at any rate something different, from anything that could be said in conceptual language. A dream only exists in the images in which it is embodied, though a shadow of its significance can be discussed for special purposes by an analyst. So it is with a myth, which exists to make actual a metaphysical, moral or psychological experience that is only potential until it has been embodied in imagery. In this respect Coleridge was more revolutionary than Wordsworth, and more fertile in his effects on the romantic age, which was seeking, among other things, a return to the poetry of creative myth after the long eighteenth-century dominance of the poetry of reasonable reflection.

Coleridge's poetic career, in its glories and in its failures, is even more extraordinary than Wordsworth's. Although Wordsworth's best poetry forms a fairly massive body, it is notorious that the best forms only a moderate proportion of the whole. I once knew a man in a prison camp who divided his copy of Wordsworth's poems into two halves, retained the first, and swapped the second for the bottom half of a pair of pyjamas. He rightly judged that the intellectual loss was very slight. Yet the process in Wordsworth is one of regular decline. His bad poetry is hardly of a different kind from his good—it is just less good. And some good poetry crops up even in the period of decline. With Coleridge it is otherwise. There are two poems, *The Ancient Mariner* and *Kubla Khan* that are unique, both in Coleridge's work and in the English language. There is one, *Christabel*, that outwardly appears to be of the same kind, but is actually a cleverly excogitated imitation. There is a handful of other good poems, *The Aeolian Harp, Frost at Midnight, Dejection* and a few others, of quite a different kind. And after that there is a considerable mass of verse, some of it a turgid waste of musing and preaching, some of it pretty and insignificant, that is fairly justly left unread by all but the most ardent Coleridgeans.

Of these *The Ancient Mariner* and *Kubla Khan* are by far the most interesting. What was happening to Coleridge when he wrote them that was never to happen again, we do not know: but the most superficial reader and the most intense student of his work can alike see that there was something. J. M. Robertson, assiduous as ever in looking for burglars under the bed, has suggested that it was the influence of opium. But Coleridge took opium almost all his life, and these particular poetic results happened only twice. *Dejection* and *The Pains of Sleep* describe its commoner effects. Clearly some unconscious mental process was at work when he wrote these two poems that was utterly different from his normal habits of mind, and far more momentous poetically. They are a perfect type of Romantic composition—meaning by romantic here something that grows according to an inner organic law, not something that is composed from outside according to a predetermined scheme.

It would be idle to pretend that we know enough about the psychology of poetic composition to explain this process. But as it happens we probably know more about the mechanism of these two poems than of any others in the language. In the first place, *The Ancient Mariner* fulfils the Coleridgean part of the joint bargain in *Lyrical Ballads*—to treat subjects "supernatural or at least romantic", but to make them credible by truth to human nature and feeling, so as to cause "that willing suspension of disbelief for the moment that constitutes poetic

faith." This might suggest the imposing of naturalistic characters on a fantastic plot—what happens for instance in Shakespeare's comedies. But this is not what happens in *The Ancient
Mariner*: there is no naturalistic character-drawing, and the
truth to human nature and feeling is of a different kind. Outwardly the most obvious thing about the poem is that it is part
of the mediaevalizing movement that had been going on since
the time of Gray. In this case the mediaeval influence at work is
that of the ballads. Percy's *Reliques*, containing a large selection
of the traditional ballad-poetry, had appeared in 1765. Literary
appreciation of the ballads had never wholly ceased, as we can
see by the references to Chevy Chase in Sidney and Addison,
but Percy inaugurated an immense revival of interest in this
popular poetry. Later editors had added to the collection, by
Coleridge's time the influence was already powerful, and it was
natural enough for a tale of strange adventure to be told in the
ballad style. This meant cutting out "characterization" and
reflection, and reducing description to bare essentials. The
archaisms of the ballad manner were more prominent in the
first edition, and were later removed; but Coleridge uses the
ballad stanza, with additions and extensions of his own; and
above all he uses the ballad manner of narration, rapid,
economical, without transitions, switching abruptly from
narrative to dialogue. Of course the poem is longer and more
highly organized than any ballad, but it retains the concrete
directness that seems to remove it from the realm of modern
self-conscious personal poetry altogether. The supernatural
passages especially, in their laconic eeriness, remind us continually of the ballad of magic and enchantment—*Thomas the
Rhymer* or *The Demon Lover*.

But, of course, the subject is not a mediaeval one at all. Its
material is drawn from the voyages of the Elizabethan seamen.
Both Wordsworth and Coleridge were great readers of books
of travel. *Shelvocke's Voyages* figure in the note to *We Are
Seven*, which gives an account of the origins of *The Ancient
Mariner*, and *Purchase's Pilgrimage* in the prefatory note to
Kubla Khan. Coleridge was actually very widely read in such
literature, and the structure of the poem is that of a typical

voyage round the Cape Horn, in which the ship, in the struggle against the westerlies, is driven to the high south latitudes, the land of ice and snow. At length they reach the Pacific, ('the silent sea' of v. 106) pick up the Trades ('the fair breeze flew': breeze—brise, the old word for trade-wind), and are finally becalmed in the equatorial Doldrums. The return is effected by purely spiritual agencies, so it would be idle to pursue the geography further.

As it happens, we have a notebook of Coleridge's with records and excerpts from his reading about this time. This has been investigated by Professor John Livingston Lowes in his book *The Road to Xanadu*, which forms the most complete and fascinating record of the genesis of a poem that we possess. There is hardly one of the most striking images of *The Ancient Mariner*, (or of its companion poem *Kubla Khan*) which cannot be traced to an original, or more commonly to several originals, in Coleridge's vast travel reading. Yet none have been transferred raw and naked, all have been transformed and fused perfectly, though it appears unconsciously, with the life of the poem as a whole. It is a supreme example of the working of the imagination in the Coleridgean sense, as we shall see in discussing his observations on that faculty in the next section. We are immensely in Professor Lowes' debt for this piece of investigation, which must have been laborious enough, yet unlike so many laborious pieces of literary research, has cast a new and brilliant light on the working of the poetic faculty. The only thing that is lacking is the sense of a directing force behind all this elaborate linking of images.[8] Professor Lowes gives us an associationist or Hartleian account of how they are linked together, but he does not attempt to tell us why. Yet if there is one impression that the *Ancient Mariner* makes, it is of completeness and organic purpose.

Can we speculate a little about what the purpose is? Wordsworth suggested that the Mariner should kill the Albatross, and that the tutelary spirits of those regions should take it upon themselves to avenge the crime:[9] and this is the formal scheme of the poem. Coleridge adds a moral—that the Mariner is "to teach, by his own example, love and reverence to all things

that God made and loveth". Mrs. Barbauld complained that
the poem had no moral, but Coleridge replied that in his
judgement it had too much.[10] However this may be, we can,
I think, be sure, as so often with Wordsworth too, that the controlling impulse of the poem is not a moral one, or not merely a
moral one; it is something more. What Wordsworth put in his
initial suggestion, what Coleridge put in the gloss quoted above,
are not what the poem is "about". In a sense this must always be
true, even of the most manufactured poem: if it can be adequately
summarized in a maxim, why write the poem? But we mean
something more than this about *The Ancient Mariner*: the poem
does not state a result, it symbolizes a process.

Untrammelled progress and untried success are symbolized
by the beginning of the voyage, and the albatross following the
ship seems to stand for the power of Nature blessing the
endeavour. Then, quite wantonly and for no reason, the
Mariner kills the albatross. The sympathy between Nature and
the voyagers is broken, and the other sailors know and feel it.
But success continues—a life cut off from the deeper springs of
energy can nevertheless run by its own momentum for a time.
Not for long, however, for on reaching the Line the ship
becomes becalmed, is afflicted with drought and stifling heat.
Natural life becomes hideous and threatening: instead of the
free and beautiful albatross,

> —slimy things did crawl with legs
> Upon a slimy sea.

The death-fires dance about the ship at night and the water
assumes strange and unnatural colours. This passage and what
follows is a powerful symbol of a life cut off by a paralysing
sense of guilt from all sympathetic natural forces, and it is the
more powerful since the horrible consequences are out of all
proportion to the objective fault. It is followed by the terrifying
episode of Death and Life-in-Death, in which Death wins
the souls of the rest of the ship's company, but Life-in-Death,
that of the Mariner himself. The reign of Life-in-Death is more
terrible than that of Death: it is the *misère de l'homme sans Dieu*

—the consciousness of being abandoned, and the utter inability to do anything for oneself towards salvation.

> The many men so beautiful
> And they all dead did lie:
> And a thousand thousand slimy things
> Lived on; and so did I.
> I looked to heaven, and tried to pray
> But or ever a prayer had gusht,
> A wicked whisper came, and made
> My heart as dry as dust.

It is a complete paralysis of the will, symbolized by the motionlessness of the ship; and in that moveless state the Mariner envies the moon and stars for their steady progress through the heavens—beautifully expressed both in the verse and the prose gloss:

> The moving moon went up the sky,
> And nowhere did abide.
> Softly she was going up,
> And a star or two beside—
>
> Her beams bemock the sultry main
> Like April hoar-frost spread;
> But where the ship's huge shadow lay
> The charmed water burnt alway
> A still and awful red.

"In his loneliness and fixedness he yearneth towards the journeying moon, and the stars that sojourn yet still move onward." And thus we approach the turning-point of the poem. The Mariner watches the water-snakes in the sea; formerly they had been slimy things, symbols of horror—but now they begin to assume a strange kind of beauty:

> Blue, glossy green and velvet black,
> They coiled and swam, and every track
> Was a flash of golden fire.

At this moment his whole feeling towards them changes: because they are alive and beautiful he blesses them.

> O happy living things, no tongue
> Their beauty might declare:
> A spring of love gushed from my heart
> And I blessed them unaware:
> Sure my kind saint took pity on me,
> And I blessed them unaware.
>
> The self-same moment I could pray;
> And from my neck so free
> The albatross fell off and sank
> Like lead into the sea.

A new peace comes into his heart and he is able to sleep again. The misery and sterility of the preceding period has been symbolized by drought (as in *The Waste Land* and the Grail legend); and now it rains. The wind begins to blow again and the ship to move. A new spiritual power takes hold of the ship and begins to guide it home. Images of the homely land-world begin to appear in the waste of waters:

> Sometimes a-dropping from the sky
> I heard the sky-lark sing;
> Sometimes all little birds that are
> How they seem to fill the sea and air
> With their sweet jargoning.
> It ceased: yet still the sails made on
> A pleasant noise till noon,
> A noise like of a hidden brook
> In the leafy month of June,
> That to the sleeping woods all night
> Singeth a quiet tune.

The regeneration of the Mariner has begun, and though he has still a long way to go, his path is now steadily homeward till he comes to his own country.

The poem is more than an allegory of guilt and regeneration.

In any ordinary sense the Mariner is very little guilty. But he has broken the bond between himself and the life of Nature, and in consequence becomes spiritually dead. What happens to him when he blesses the water-snakes in the tropical calm is a psychic rebirth—a rebirth that must at times happen to all men and all cultures unless they are to dry up in a living death. The whole poem is indeed a vivid presentation of the rebirth myth as it is conceived by Jung[11]—the psychologist who has done most to explain these recurrent forms of imaginative literature. But such explanations of poetry are not convincing to everyone and are not easily demonstrable, so I will not labour the point. What we must explain is that it is not the final "moral", it is the living symbolization of this universal psychic experience that gives the poem its lasting power. It is as though Coleridge tapped a deeper level of consciousness here than he was ever to reach again.

Kubla Khan has the same quality of enchantment, but it is more puzzling, partly because it is a fragment, but for another reason, too—it is a fragment of a private experience, not of a universal one. Its origin is well known. It was composed in an opium dream;[12] and before it could all be written out "a person on business from Porlock" interrupted the poet at his task, and when he returned to it, as commonly happens with dreams, all was gone. An immediate inspiration was again in a book of voyages that Coleridge was reading just before he fell asleep; and Livingston Lowes has shown that echoes from many other travels are found in its short fifty lines. But here it would be harder to look for the controlling purpose; if there was one, it was in Coleridge's private biography, in a region that was not accessible to his own inspection, and is still less to ours. Only a poet with a mind like Coleridge's, as sensitive as his own Aeolian harp, could catch the dream-images in all their strangeness and authenticity, and the abiding fascination of the poem is that it is a fragment of psychic life of a kind which in the nature of things is rarely communicable to the outside world. Writing of this kind, without the usual logical and conceptual framework is sometimes called 'pure poetry'; it is not readily susceptible to analysis, except perhaps of a psychological kind.

However, this is not wholly impossible. The poem as it
stands does present a meaning, consistent both with itself and
with what we know of Coleridge's mind. The fact that a poem
is not wholly or certainly explicable should not discourage us
from explaining it as well as we can. The opening lines, suggested by a passage in Purchas's *Pilgrimage*, that Coleridge
was reading as he entered his dream or reverie, describes an
ideal landscape watered by a sacred river, of paradisal happiness, in which Kubla is such an all-powerful lord that he can
create his pleasure-dome by mere decree. But in the succeeding
lines (12–30) come images of fear, enchantment, violent and
uncontrollable energy, oblivion and death and forebodings of
strife. The paradisal landscape is cleft by a chasm which is
savage and fearsome, and from it a mighty fountain is forced,
throwing up huge rocks: and the fountain turns out to be the
sacred river itself, bursting out after an underground sojourn,
like the classical Alpheus, from which its name Alph seems to
be derived. It flows for a little in the open, then disappears
for good. And Kubla hears prophecies of war. The idyllic
calm of the opening lines is threatened, and the movements of
Alph seem to echo or symbolize this. Lines 31–6 add little,
but bring us back to the pleasure-dome, show it reflected in
the river, and bring it closely into contact both with the
fountain (uncontrolled bounding energy) and the caves (final
annihilation).

Then we come to the last eighteen lines, of which Lowes
said "the pageant is as aimless as it is magnificent." And here
is the most characteristic dream-feature of the poem—the
sudden switch from Kubla and the Xanadu landscape. The
poet now speaks in his own person and has a vision of an
Abyssinian maid singing of Mount Abora. Mount Abora is
Milton's Mount Amara (so written in an earlier manuscript),
and Mount Amara is a fabled paradise, as we can see by
consulting *Paradise Lost*, IV, 268–84. So the Abyssinian maid
is singing of a paradisal landscape very like that of the opening
lines—singing in fact of the same cluster of ideas under a
different name and guise. And (42–54) if he, the poet, could
re-live in his imagination her song, he himself could build the

magic pleasure-dome, as Kubla had done, he himself could become what Kubla was, a figure of power, of mystery and enchantment.

Explanation could be pushed much farther. This is enough to suggest that the poem, for all its dream-like air, is not unintelligible as Lowes suggests; and that what underlies it is the recurrent Coleridgean theme of poetic inspiration. Alph, the sacred river is surely the river of the Muses, the poetic imagination itself, which is terrible as well as seductive, and threatened ultimately with conflict and extinction, as Coleridge later was too bitterly to know. Could he only recapture at will the vision of it, and the paradise through which it flows, all his dreamed-of poetry would get written and he would become the inspired magical prophet-bard which the quintessential romantic poet asks to be.

Christabel was intended for inclusion in Lyrical Ballads— but like so many of Coleridge's projects it was not finished in time, and in the end was never finished at all. Coleridge always said he knew exactly how it was to go on, but was never revisited by the creative impulse to finish it. A summary of the conclusion made by a friend does actually exist. But one suspects in this case, as perhaps in that of Keat's *Hyperion*, that the defect was ultimately structural. If it had been conceived as a whole it would have been finished. It is a tale of chivalry and magic, somewhat like Scott's lays, and it may actually have influenced them, for although it was written before and not published till after them, Scott had heard it read in manuscript. This suggests a common ancestry—and we are probably to find it in the ballads, and the Gothic romances that had been fashionable since Horace Walpole. It is an accomplished example of that less profound side of the romantic movement to which, in their different ways, *The Lady of the Lake*, *The Eve of St. Agnes* and Morris's romances all belong—the use of mediaeval themes for their beauty or mystery or enchantment, without any other very strong reason for the choice. The difference between this poem and *The Ancient Mariner* is very marked, in spite of superficial resemblances. *The Ancient Mariner* seems to come as it comes, a complete conception, in response to some very deep inner experience; while *Christabel* is a haunting piece of romantic composition, but definitely composition; its elements are not so much symbols as stage properties, and the setting, instead of being the inevitable environment for such a story, is an exquisite piece of *décor*. It is notable that Professor Lowes found it quite impossible to include *Christabel* in his study—or rather that *Christabel* obstinately refused to include itself. Whatever the process by which it was constructed, it was different from that which went to the making of *The Ancient Mariner* and *Kubla Khan*.

Nevertheless, it contains some of Coleridge's best verse—some enchanting vignettes in the romantic taste in the first part; and in the second the fine passage about the broken friendship between Roland and Sir Leoline, a passage that probably derives a good deal of its force from an estrangement that had come about between Coleridge and his friend Lamb. Coleridge announces that the verse is not, as it seems, irregular, but is founded on a new principle—that of counting the accents instead of the syllables. This is supposed to be a landmark in the romantic emancipation of verse-form. Actually what Coleridge is doing is not so new as he supposes: he is varying his rhythm, extremely subtly and beautifully, but in a way that would not have been very startling before the eighteenth-century insistence on strict syllabic regularity. Rather than doing anything new, he is returning to a use of the full metrical resources of English that had been normal in the sixteenth and seventeenth centuries.

The rest of Coleridge's poetry is mostly discursive and reflective. The big pieces of his early years, *Religious Musings* and *The Destiny of Nations* are intolerably turgid and long-winded. He could at all times throw off harmonious and distinguished scraps of verse, and some of these coalesced into poems. Some are idyllic and domestic, like the early *Aeolian Harp, This Lime-Tree Bower* and *Frost at Midnight*. They are too diffuse and unorganized to make a very decisive total impression, but all contain lines and passages, descriptive, reflective and reminiscent, that breathe out the peculiar air of soft, delicate yet eager intelligence that is Coleridge's normal endowment. *Love* and *Lewti* are pretty trifles. *France: an Ode* is chiefly interesting for its account of Coleridge's relation to the Revolution—a more vehement engagement and a more sudden disillusionment than Wordsworth's, and both less profound in their emotional effects. The greatest and most terrible of these poems is the *Ode on Dejection*, written in 1802: almost the swan-song of Coleridge's poetic career. It is a profoundly melancholy account of the state of nerveless hopelessness to which Coleridge had been reduced by ill-health, opium and domestic misfortune. He projects his own feelings into the stormy and moonlit night around him, finding in these natural forms a symbol of his own emotion, as Shelley does in the *Ode to the West Wind*. The descriptive passages are exquisite in their accuracy of observation—almost as though Ruskin had been writing them in verse: and the poem as a whole is unforgettable for its profound sadness. It is a description in other terms of the state in which the Ancient Mariner found himself when alone and becalmed in the tropical sea: but alas, the reviving rain and wind were never to visit Coleridge again except in the rarest and most fitful gusts.

iii. POETIC DICTION AND IMAGINATION

One of the fullest commentaries on *Lyrical Ballads* and the poetry of its period is provided by Wordsworth and Coleridge themselves. Wordsworth's explanation of his own objects in various prefaces and essays, Coleridge's commentary on his own and Wordsworth's career in *Biographia Literaria*, are among the most celebrated documents of the time. Whether they deserve their reputation or not is another matter: they certainly provide an indispensable appendix to the original creative work; and they did a good deal to set the course of poetry for the whole of the nineteenth century. The effect of Wordsworth's critical doctrines is indeed not exhausted yet; though there are probably few poets today who are directly under his influence, many of the feelings about diction and poetic ornament that now seem almost instinctive are the direct result of the Words-worthian reforms.

Wordsworth's prose writings are more voluminous than we might expect, and Coleridge gave a mass of literary lectures, surviving in various states of preservation, which we shall not deal with here. The vital part is the Preface and Appendix to *Lyrical Ballads*, first published in 1800 and revised in 1802; and Coleridge's critique of this, and of Wordsworth's work in general, in *Biographia Literaria* (1817). The whole is commonly regarded as a controversy between Wordsworth and Coleridge on the subject of poetic diction, and has acquired a sinister familiarity as an examination subject. This is unfortunate, since it tends to reduce the argument to a dreary tagging off of points where Coleridge disagreed with Wordsworth and was right—or wrong, as the case may be—to the neglect of other and more interesting aspects of their criticism. In fact, they were hardly talking about the same things. Criticism of poetry may be either original exploration, or the providing of maps and sign-posts for later travellers. Wordsworth's was of the first kind—a clearing of the ground for his own new work; he is concerned with what happens, or should happen, in the poet's mind in the act of composition. Coleridge, in these passages at any rate, is concerned with the *fait accompli*, with what happens in the reader's mind in the act of appreciation or judgement. Coleridge had a far more analytical mind, and was in any case writing after the event with the finished products before him. Naturally, he has the best of the argument, if we are to regard it as an argument. But perhaps that is not the most fruitful way of looking at this body of critical writing. It is rather an explora-tion, from two slightly different angles, of the widening possi-bilities of poetry.

The immediate purpose of Wordsworth's preface is to defend his poems against the charges of lowness and unpoetical-ness that had been made against both their subjects and their diction. Its wider intention is to relate poetry as closely as possible to common life, to remove it in the first place from the realm of fantasy, and in the second from that of polite or over-sophisti-cated amusement. He speaks therefore of "the gaudiness and inane phraseology of many modern writers", of neglect of the older literature in favour of "frantic novels, sickly stupid German tragedies, and deluges of idle and extravagant stories in verse". Poetry should be "the spontaneous overflow of powerful feelings", not the mere satisfaction of a taste for imagery and ornament. A historical critic might object that the feelings that inspire poetry need not be powerful, and that the overflow may be considerably less than spontaneous—unless we are to deny *The Rape of the Lock* and *Lycidas* the title of poetry: but Wordsworth's criticism, like that of most imaginative writers, is an indication of his own purpose, and we value it less for judicial impartiality than for its statement of the most powerful creative purpose of the time. Wordsworth's aim in all this is to show the poet as a man appealing to the normal interests of mankind, not as a peculiar being appealing to a specialized taste.

"He is a man speaking to men: a man, it is true, endowed with more lively sensibility, more enthusiasm and tenderness, who has a greater knowledge of human nature, and a more comprehensive soul, than are supposed to be common among mankind; a man pleased with his own passions and volitions, and who rejoices more than other men in the spirit of life that is in him; delighted to contemplate similar volitions and passions as manifested in the goings-on of the Universe, and habitually impelled to create them where he does not find them."

The poet's pleasure in his art is an acknowledgement of the beauty of the world. So is the work of the scientist, but his is an indirect and laborious pleasure, hard to come by and hard to transmit: while the poet comes "singing a song in which all human beings join with him".

"In spite of difference of soil and climate, of language and manners, of laws and customs: in spite of things silently gone out of mind, and things violently destroyed; the Poet binds together by passion and knowledge the vast empire of human society, as it is spread over the whole earth and over all time."

Wordsworth's argument, which is here at its most passionate and deeply felt, is that poetry is the concrete, the immediately experienced part of knowledge, in which the sensations and the emotions can join. Those who suppose that Wordsworth would confine the commerce of the poet to hills and sheep, and that the advent of an urban and scientific age means some sort of anti-Wordsworthian revolution (the notion was vaguely current in the 1930s) should note the passage that follows.

"If the labours of the men of science should ever create any material revolution, direct or indirect, in our condition, and in the impressions which we habitually receive, the Poet will sleep then no more than at present; he will be ready to follow the steps of the man of science, not only in those general indirect effects, but he will be at his side, carrying sensation into the midst of the objects of the science itself. The remotest discoveries of the Chemist, the Botanist, or Mineralogist, will be as proper objects of the Poet's art as any upon which it can be employed, if the time shall ever come when these things shall be familiar to us, and the relations under which they are contemplated by the followers of these respective sciences shall be manifestly and palpably material to us as enjoying and suffering beings. If the time should ever come when what is now called science, thus familiarized to men, shall be ready to put on, as it were, a form of flesh and blood, the Poet will lend his divine spirit to aid the transfiguration, and will welcome the Being thus produced as a dear and genuine inmate of the household of man."

Surveying the poetry and the science of the present, we can hardly say that that stage has been reached: the remarkable thing about these lines, written in 1802, is that they can provide so adequate a faith for succeeding ages, that they realize so clearly the difficulty of incorporating science into our imaginative life, yet still believe that it can be accomplished. Wordsworth here shows himself possessed of a conception of poetry that quite transcends the limits of his own time and temperament.

As for the subjects of his poetry, Wordsworth emphasizes their psychological and moral interests in order to defend them from the charges of triviality and false simplicity that had been made against them. He is not after all trying to write familiar anecdotes or nursery tales; he is seeking the fundamentals of human life by contemplating its simplest forms. We are not asked to be interested in Michael because he is a picturesque character, peculiar by his station or calling, but because he is a man, revealing in their least elaborated form passions common to all men. Wordsworth is quite different from the rural poet who seeks to focus attention on the peculiarities of a special class or district; and it is in an attempt to make this plain that he talks of tracing in his familiar incidents "the primary laws of our nature". It is only in sudden flashes that Wordsworth becomes possessed of the piercing mystical intuition of Blake:

> To see a World in a Grain of Sand
> And a Heaven in a Wild Flower,
> Hold infinity in the palm of your hand
> And Eternity in an hour:

and when this happens he rarely comments on it. The part of his poetry that he can explain is the more pedestrian part where he is, or believes himself to be, abstracting general laws from familiar instances.

Behind the question of poetic diction, then, more fundamental than any technical problem, is the fact that he is predisposed to his familiar themes for moral and psychological reasons. What he says is that

> "Humble and rustic life was generally chosen, because, in that condition, the essential passions of the heart find a better soil in which they can attain their maturity, are less under restraint and speak a plainer and more emphatic language; . . . because the manners of rural life . . . are more durable; and, lastly, because in that condition the passions of men are incorporated with the beautiful and permanent forms of nature."

An utterance which combines, in typically Wordsworthian

proportions, the values of the eighteenth century with those of the Romantic age. The search for the permanent and the durable merely repeats, in other language, the Augustan principle of "following Nature", which, as a critical precept, means simply this. But, like other categorical imperatives, the command "follow Nature" turns out to be a formal principle without a clear material content. To follow Nature is to look for what is fundamental and unchanging in human life: but what *is* fundamental? It has often been remarked that every literary revolution announces itself as a return to nature. It is in Wordsworth's answer to this question that he is most typical of his own age. To some, the foundations of human nature are to be found in the grand passions of the noblest of mankind; to others in the metaphysical relation of man to God; to Wordsworth they are "the simple primary affections and duties", seen at their clearest in peasant life because it contains so little else. He could hardly have been so sure of this if the work of Rousseau had not prepared his generation for a revolt against sophistication, an idealization of simplicity. But Wordsworth's conviction was not obtained at second hand; it was a part, of course, of the revolutionary and democratic sentiment that had absorbed his young manhood; but still more it was a part of the normal everyday experience of his childhood years. We all tend to feel that the people we have been brought up with are somehow more real than other varieties of the human race; and to Wordsworth it was the "shepherds, dwellers in our valleys" that continued to represent essential humanity.

It is from this root that his technical interest in the language of simple life naturally springs. If real humanity is to be found among simple people this also is the place to look for real human speech. And the equation between this and the proper language of poetry is to Wordsworth a perfectly obvious one. It will not necessarily be so to other people. Wordsworth quite evidently believes that a poem moves the reader in the same way as the experience it describes would have done, if it were encountered in real life. He even believes that a poem is the more moving the more closely it reproduces the language of the persons concerned in the actual experience.

"However exalted a notion we wish to cherish of the character of the Poet, it is obvious, that while he describes and imitates passions, his employment is in some degree mechanical, compared with the freedom and power of real and substantial action and suffering. So that it will be the wish of the Poet to bring his own feelings near to those of the persons whose feelings he describes . . . and, the more industriously he applies this principle, the deeper will be his faith that no word, which *his* fancy or imagination can suggest, will be to be compared with those which are the emanations of reality and truth."

However, Wordsworth has enough historic sense to realize obscurely that this is not in fact what poets in general have felt, that most poetry has not been written on this principle, and that experiment is therefore necessary to see whether it will work. His statement of his case varies in different places, and it is hardly worth while to stand too much on verbal niceties, since his general object is clear enough. The Advertisement to L.B. says that the majority of the poems were written "Chiefly with a view to ascertain how far the language of conversation in the middle and lower classes of society is adapted to the purposes of poetic pleasure". The preface later describes the chosen diction as "a selection of language really used by men"; which is something rather different. The class aspect disappears, and the word "selection" allows the elimination of local and social peculiarities. This seems to imply that the principle is mainly negative; Wordsworth's main object is not so much to include the vernacular as to cut out all language that might *not* be used in ordinary speech. And this impression is confirmed when we turn to the poems themselves. There is nowhere in Wordsworth the slightest attempt to reproduce the actual turns of speech common in humble and rustic life. He never attempts dialect poetry in the manner of, say, William Barnes; nor does he try to base a literary language on an actual peasant speech, like Synge. He does not even enrich his language with the occasional salty colloquialism; and no one who knows Northern dialect could find him sensitive to its peculiar qualities. In fact his real worry is not about common speech: it is to come to some sort of terms with established poetic diction, as we can see in the appendix to the preface of 1802. His historical account of how this poetic diction arose has been quoted above in the chapter on Gray. It is, within its limits, admirable, and is a just criticism of the vices of a style like that of Gray's odes. That Wordsworth had Gray in mind is shown by his quotation of the sonnet on the death of West, somewhat unfairly and summarily dealt with, and his mention of Gray in the same passage as "at the head of those who, by their reasonings, have attempted to widen the space of separation between Prose and Metrical composition". But his argument here still depends on the belief that a poem affects us as the incident it describes affects him who experienced it. Wordsworth never realizes that a poem is a new creation, not merely a representation of something that has existed in the actual world. He never realizes that words derive their power from their associations, that language is like a long-inhabited historic site, with the successive deposits of all cultural levels embedded in it. His theory would be perfect if every poet came new into a world with no previous poetry behind him. But it does not account at all for the growth of a tradition of poetic language, rich in memories and associations. To take a few obvious examples, it does not account for Anglo-Saxon poetry, with its large vocabulary of "kennings"—special phrases and names reserved for poetry alone; it does not account for Elizabethan verse, enriched with all the gorgeous lumber of the Renaissance; it does not account for Milton—whose language is often almost incomprehensible without some sensibility to its learned overtones. But why go on? Anyone could supply with five minutes' thought half a dozen passages that would destroy the general application of Wordsworth's doctrine. And the partial quotations, the truisms and the illogical deductions by which it is supported do not inspire any great confidence. But the refutation of these can be safely left to Coleridge.

He passes on to the consideration of metre. He foresees that he may be asked "Why, professing these opinions, he has written in verse." To this his first answer is that metre is a "superadded pleasure" to the other virtues of good writing.

But it is succeeded by a more analytical attempt to explain the function of metre. Wordsworth finds it in the attempt to find a bounding, regularizing influence to contain the excitement of passion. He argues here extremely ingeniously, and with considerable psychological subtlety, to show the effect of metre in making bearable the kind of scenes which are almost unbearably affecting in prose—that the moving passages of *Clarissa* really distress us, "while Shakespeare's writings, in the most pathetic scenes, never act upon us, as pathetic, beyond the bounds of pleasure—an effect which, in a much greater degree than might at first be imagined, is to be ascribed to small, but continual and regular impulses of pleasurable surprise from the metrical arrangement". It is hardly possible to ascribe this effect mainly to the metre: but Wordsworth's intention is clearly to present metre as one of the forces that remove the passions of poetry to a suitable "aesthetic distance", and so make them in themselves a source of pleasure. In prose form these emotions are brought closer to us, and so press more heavily on the sympathies.

In spite of inconsistencies of detail, the motive force of the preface is evident enough. It is an exposition of Wordsworth's poetic creed, and it is chiefly open to attack because it makes a statement of his own practice in the form of a statement about poetry at large. This is the burden of Coleridge's reply. It is found at length in *Biographia Literaria*, Chapter IV, and in Chapters XIV to XXII. He points out at the beginning that Wordsworth's poems would hardly have been attacked if it had not been for the challenging and dubious statements in the Preface. If Coleridge's aim had been merely to confute Wordsworth he could have done so simply enough by taking examples from existing poetry, as F. L. Lucas has vigorously pointed out.[13] "There neither is, nor can be, any essential difference between the language of prose and metrical composition." The way to confute universal negatives of this kind is to produce contrary examples. But it is against Coleridge's nature to proceed in this manner. He prefers to argue from general principles. For he is not writing to contradict or confute, but to do something more serious—to disentangle the essential and important truth from the difficulties created by Wordsworth's less philosophical utterance.

In the first place, he attacks the illusions about the language of rustic life, and finds it easy to demonstrate that such a language, purged from local and class peculiarities, is no different from any other language, except as it is more limited in its range. He shows, with copious illustrations, that the virtues of neutral and unelaborated simplicity are by no means those of the most striking passages of Wordsworth's own poetry. He points out that Wordsworth's proposition that there is a large part of the language of poetry which differs in no way from that of prose is not convertible; it does not show, what alone requires to be shown, that there is *no* part of the language of poetry that differs from that of prose. And he argues from the effects of metre. Metre arouses in the reader certain expectations of a language different from the ordinary. "I write in metre *because* I am going to use a language different from that of prose." Though this is little more true as a general statement than Wordsworth's own, and Coleridge goes on to contradict himself in the next chapter where he shows, quite rightly, that there is a neutral style, or one common to both prose and poetry. His argument is more logical, more analytical than Wordsworth's, but still not wholly satisfactory as a piece of dialectic. Its main merit is that it produces by the way the earliest, and still one of the fullest and most penetrating analyses of the peculiar excellences of Wordsworth's verse.

Nevertheless, the marks on our literature have been permanent. "Gaudiness and inane phraseology", at least of the type of which Wordsworth was talking, now finally disappear. Attention is focused on the relation of poetry to living speech —a relation which is not so simple as Wordsworth supposed, which had been discovered in practice long before his day, but which he first brought into the critical limelight. If we were asked to amend Wordsworth's and Coleridge's conclusions in the light of current critical opinion we should have to pay as much attention to rhythm as they do to vocabulary: we now realize more clearly that "the language really used by men" is not merely a matter of the choice of words—which is Wordsworth's chief concern; or even of word-order, which to Coleridge seems at least as important: it is a matter of the whole run and movement of the sentence, its structure and its pauses. We realize that the living speech of the age is a constant source of vitality to poetry; but that living speech cannot be simply "fitted to metrical arrangement", as Wordsworth puts it; the life of verse springs from an ever-present but ever-varying tension between the rhythm of current speech and the formal metrical scheme. And there is a similar varying tension between the language of the age and the language of poetry. Sometimes the two come very close together; if they remain too close for too long the result is an unimaginative limitation of the themes and emotions with which poetry can deal. For we expect poetry to cope with experiences more intense and more subtle than those which "the language of the age" meets with every day. Commonly, after a time of approximation they tend to diverge; if the divergence goes too far and lasts too long the danger is that poetry develops a factitious dialect divorced from the current springs of life. Almost any statement about the relation between the two languages *may* be true, at some stage in the process. Gray's "the language of the age is never the language of poetry" was written when poetry had had a surfeit of rational discourse in a polished conversational style: Wordsworth's pronouncements when it had had a surfeit of the "cumbrous splendours" of Gray. Each was justified in its day: but to make any statement of the matter that is generally true is more complicated than either of them suspected. Perhaps we are often mistaken in trying to judge such critical pronouncements in the light of eternity—for their real function was to indicate the next thing to be done.

This brings up the whole question of Coleridge's speculative and philosophical criticism. More than any other critic he makes the constant attempt to base his judgements on general principles—and not only critical principles, but epistemological and ultimately metaphysical ones. The enterprise is obviously one to be admired; but it has created obstacles which his less strenuous successors have often been unwilling to surmount. However, one is apt to find at the end that Coleridge's definitions and distinctions have survived, that his conclusions remain active among minds that have never troubled to look into the processes by which they were reached. Half the nineteenth century was taught to think by Coleridge, as John Stuart Mill remarked; and there is a certain impertinence in thus neglecting the mental processes of one whose equipment was so formidable and whose influence was so immense.

Many of Coleridge's elaborately philosophical definitions turn out to be of direct literary value. Such is the definition of a poem in Chapter XIV of *Biographia*. The attempt seems unpromising enough, and we are not encouraged by the opening passage on "the office of philosophical disquisition". Coleridge begins by noting the obvious distinction of metre and rhyme, pointing out that it may be used for merely mnemonic purposes (as in the gender rhymes, "Thirty days hath September", etc.), but that even in these lowly forms the regular recurrence of sounds and quantities (if he is speaking of English verse he means stresses) gives a certain pleasure of its own. But a further distinction between a poem and other kinds of writing is the difference of object. The immediate object may be the communication of truths, as in works of science or history. But in a poem this is not the immediate object; the immediate object is the communication of pleasure. The word pleasure here perhaps needs further analysis, but the term is traditional, and we may agree that the distinction is a valid one. The communication of pleasure, however, may be the object of works not metrically composed, such as novels and prose romances, which no one has ever attempted to call poems. Suppose one cast these into metrical form, would they then become poems? No; because the metre would be a mere meaningless addition, and "nothing can permanently please, which does not contain in itself the reason why it is so and not otherwise." The regular recurrence of accent and sound in metre excite a perpetual and distinct attention to each part. We cannot read a poem by merely skimming through it to get the general gist, as we can a newspaper article. On this basis then we can work out a final definition.

"A poem is that species of composition, which is opposed

to works of science by having for its immediate object pleasure, not truth; and from all other species—(having this object in common with it)—it is discriminated by proposing to itself such delight from the whole, as is compatible with a distinct gratification from each component part."

It would be a great mistake for the pure "literary" critic to object that this is mere arid argument in general terms, without reference to actual poems. It is of course based on long experience of poems and poetry, which Coleridge does not at the moment choose to bring into the foreground. The test is whether the general statement can be usefully applied to actual poetry. We often do not realize the value of Coleridge's distinctions because we do not seek to use them in practice. When we do we are apt to find their value soon enough. This definition of a poem, often passed over, is in fact one of the most pregnant of critical utterances. It contains the germ of the modern distinction between "scientific" and "emotive" language; and the germ therefore of much later discussion of poetry and science, poetry and belief. And in the final sentence—that poetry demands attention, not only to the whole, but to each individual part, we surely have the ultimate distinction between prose and poetry, a criterion which overrides that of mere metre, which explains our obstinate tendency to class the more consciously rhythmical kinds of prose with poetry; which, properly understood, leads on, not to hair-splitting and abstraction, but to that close attention to texture and imagery that the proper reading of poetry demands. It is easy to class abstract and general criticism of this kind as mere word-spinning: at its best it is not so: it removes us for a time from the purely literary field, but only in order that we may understand it the better when we return to it.

By far the most celebrated of Coleridge's essays in this direction is his distinction between Fancy and Imagination. This has been variously discussed—first from the strictly philosophical point of view, its relation to the thought of the German idealists, Kant and Schelling, who exercised such a profound influence on Coleridge's mature philosophical ideas. This lies outside our field. Much labour has been wasted in discussing whether there "really" is any such distinction. Many pure critics have written the whole thing off as a piece of transcendental mystification. But literary critics can be wrong; and in England they have often been so because they are unable or unwilling to relate literary judgements to other departments of thought. Let us first try to discover as simply as we can what Coleridge meant.

We may admit at the start that those who accuse Coleridge of mystery-making are given a good deal of justification. We first hear of the Imagination-Fancy distinction in Chapter IV of *Biographia*, in connection with Wordsworth's poetry, of which Imagination is said to be the dominant quality. We are promised a full explanation of it. There follow five chapters intended as a preliminary explanation of the foundation of Coleridge's philosophical beliefs, including his confutation of Hartley's association theory and an account of his own debt to the German idealists, especially Kant, Fichte and Schelling. Of the philosophical merits of these chapters I am not qualified to speak, but they are of course vital as an account of the growth of one of the most influential minds of the century. There follows (a typical, and maddening, Coleridgean trick) two chapters of mere digression. And thus we reach Chapter XII, which announces itself as a preliminary exhortation to those who propose to study the distinction that is about to be made. Its most significant part is Coleridge's attempt to find a secure basis for all our knowledge. This he discovers in the act of self-consciousness, the act of saying I AM, for that alone depends on no outside object; subject and object, that which knows and that which is known here being perfectly united. God's self-consciousness, his recognition of his own being, is the primary creative act of the universe. Chapter XIII then holds out to us the promise of discussing "The Imagination or Esemplastic power" itself. But alas! the prospect turns out to be a mirage; at the moment when the secret is about to be revealed there is interposed a fatal letter from a friend (a mythical friend, one of

Coleridge's other selves) advising him not to communicate so strange a truth to a world unprepared to receive it. And we are put off with the two paragraphs that follow.

"The imagination then I consider as either primary, or secondary. The primary imagination I hold to be the living power and prime agent of all human perception, and as a repetition in the finite mind of the eternal act of creation in the infinite I AM. The secondary I consider as an echo of the former, co-existing with the conscious will, yet still as identical with the primary in the kind of its agency, and differing only in degree, and in the mode of its operation. It dissolves, diffuses, dissipates, in order to re-create; or where this process is rendered impossible, yet still, at all events, it struggles to idealize and to unify. It is essentially vital, even as all objects (as objects) are essentially fixed and dead.

"Fancy, on the contrary, has no other counters to play with but fixities and definites. The Fancy is indeed no other than a mode of memory emancipated from the order of time and space; and blended with, and modified by that empirical phenomenon of the will, which we express by the word choice. But equally with the ordinary memory, it must receive all its materials ready-made from the law of association."

The reader who wishes for a full discussion of this passage, its genesis and its bearings, must be referred elsewhere.[14] Let us here attempt something much more modest. The primary imagination is then the act of self-consciousness referred to above as the foundation of all knowledge and all perception. It is literally the act by which each one of us creates his world, and is a human repetition of the act by which God created the world as a whole. The secondary imagination is the poetic imagination, with which we are here specially concerned. Just as the primary imagination unites the knower and the known in a single act, so the secondary or poetic imagination unites the poet's mind with the objects of its contemplation, and these various objects with each other. It is that which makes a poem, not merely a reproduction of things previously existing in the objective world, but a new unity, with an existence of its own. How it does so is best described in the words Coleridge uses of Wordsworth's poetry; it is by

"The union of deep feeling with profound thought; the fine balance of truth in observing, with the imaginative faculty in modifying, the objects observed; and, above all, the original gift of spreading the tone, the atmosphere, and with it the depth and height of the ideal world, around forms, incidents and situations of which, for the common view, custom had bedimmed all the lustre and dried up the sparkle and the dewdrops."

It is this power then that makes the figure of the Leech-gatherer something more than a mere remembered old man, and Tintern Abbey something more than a remembered landscape. In both detached material reminiscences are made into new wholes under the pressure of a powerful impulse of feeling. Fancy merely recombines existing things in a new way; if it produces a unity it is that of a mixture, not that of a chemical compound. Often it is playful; compare the sentimental assembly of recollected fragments in Rupert Brooke's *Grantchester* with the Wordsworthian treatment of a remembered landscape. Yet the difference is not one of seriousness, it is a different kind of thinking.

> Mark you the floor? that square and speckled stone,
>> Which looks so firm and strong,
>>> Is Patience:
> And the other black and grave, wherewith each one
>> Is checker'd all along,
>>> Humility:
> The gentle rising, which on either hand
>> Leads to the quire above,
>>> Is Confidence:
> But the sweet cement, which in one sure band
>> Ties the whole frame, is Love
>>> And Charity.

The gentle gravity of these lines of Herbert's (from *The*

Church Floor) is wholly serious in intention; yet it remains a fanciful, not an imaginative way of thinking. When Herbert's imagination awakes the effect is quite different; as in the closing lines of *The Collar*:

> But as I raved, and grew more fierce and wild
>   At every word,
> Methought I heard one calling "Child":
>   And I replied, "My Lord!"

The application of the distinction to imagery has been indicated by Coleridge himself[15] and exhaustively discussed by I. A. Richards. But the principal significance of the Coleridgean concept of Imagination is not in this field, not in its use as a tool in the analysis of styles and images. It is in the connexion between the secondary and the primary imagination. If the poet's imagination is an echo, an analogy of the act which is the foundation of all knowledge and all perception, it occupies a more central position in the scheme of things than had hitherto been suspected. The poets had been revered before as leaders and teachers of mankind—but only because they provided living examples of virtues that were known without them; at worst they had been respected as honest entertainers. Coleridge's theory implies a claim that the poet is in possession of a voluntary power, which is in some sense one not only with the power that is active in all human perception, but is even a human analogy to the creative power of God. This is to exalt the position of the poetic imagination very high indeed, and to exalt the poet into a man with some special insight into the nature of things. It is no longer his duty to follow Nature by following the Ancients; he has private access to the secrets of Nature, because he is working by a power analogous to hers. Whether or in what sense this belief is true, we need not discuss. But we must record it as a historical phenomenon; for it forms the ideological foundation of romantic poetry. We can see in it the beginning of a split between the poet and the man of the world that was unknown to the eighteenth century, and that has

grown steadily more acute till our own day. The poet assumes
the rôle of the prophet; and a stiff-necked and uncircumcised
generation retaliates by reducing him to a social misfit; till at the
close of the nineteenth century the poets retort upon the world
by trying to cut art off from its social roots altogether. But this
is for the future; in the Romantic age itself the Coleridgean
doctrine of imagination provides the philosophic background
for Shelley's dictum "Poets are the unacknowledged legislators
of the world".

One of the critical results of this faith is illustrated in
Coleridge's Shakespeare criticism. To the eighteenth-century
critics, Shakespeare had been a poet, pre-eminent among his
fellows, but still a man as other men are, capable of lapses and
errors. To Coleridge, Shakespeare is the supreme example of a
central and supremely important faculty, and begins therefore
to assume almost superhuman status. His lightest inconsistencies, his most obvious lapses of attention are not to be
accounted for as we account for other human frailties, but to be
justified as we justify the works of God to man. It is the beginning of Shakespeare idolatry—an exaggerated reverence which
has been compensated in our day by a rather too self-con-
sciously down-to-earth approach. There are some bad lapses
into rigmarole and unctuousness in Coleridge's Shakespeare
criticism; and they inspire at times a passing wish for the few
clear concepts, the steady common sense of Johnson.

But it is only a passing wish. The work that could be done
with the Johnsonian apparatus had been done. Augustan
criticism had become a standing pool. Coleridge came to
trouble the waters, and his operations, like those of the angel,
brought an access of life and strength. His philosophy is the
intellectual centre of the Romantic movement, and his criticism
is a part of his philosophy. The artistic imagination is only one
instance of a power by which the dead mechanistic world of
later eighteenth-century thought was to be revived. *Biographia
Literaria* must be supplemented by *Aids to Reflection* and *The
Friend* if it is to be fully understood. It will not yield to impatient reading, but it is a book to which the serious student of
poetry must constantly return, often to find new light in

places that before seemed exceedingly obscure. Gradually one comes to realize the unity of Coleridge's thought, and the strength that his criticism derives from the depth and range of his philosophic interests.

iv. LATER YEARS

Almost the last momentous change in Wordsworth's outward life was the return to his own Lake country in 1799. Alfoxden saw the genesis of *Lyrical Ballads*, but Wordsworth's life was not re-established on its permanent foundations until he went back to Westmorland and settled with Dorothy at Town End at Grasmere. This was to be his home for the next eight years. and it is here that most of the poems of his great period were written. The daily life of the Wordsworths in these peaceful and productive years can best be seen in Dorothy's journals; and its dominant emotional experiences both in the Westmorland eclogues like *Michael* and *The Brothers*, and the many smaller pieces, especially those written between 1800 and 1803. The major record, however, of the emotions with which they returned to their own country is to be found in the fragment of *The Recluse*—not published till 1888, long after Wordsworth's death: but apparently written for the most part in 1800.[16] Apart from *The Excursion*, it is all that was completed of the great tripartite work that he had planned at the beginning of his career. This rather shadowy project dominated the central years of Wordsworth's life. But there is a significant change of tone between *The Recluse* of 1800 and *The Excursion* of 1814; and the change betrays the passing over of the young Wordsworth into the middle-aged man who commands less of our interest and sympathy.

The fragment of *The Recluse* consists largely of a description of the vale of Grasmere where they had come to live. It is filled with a radiant sense of homecoming, of complete participation both in the natural life of the place, and in the life of the other dwellers in the valley. It is the perfect appendix to *The Prelude*, but it is not a conclusion. It is at once a return to early pieties and the start of something new. Apart from the joy in natural loveliness, perhaps the most important feeling in it is the sense of being again among one's own people, of belonging, by every tie of affection and proximity, to a natural society.

> we do not tend a lamp
> Whose lustre we alone participate,
> Which shines dependent upon us alone,
> Mortal, though bright, a dying, dying flame.
> Look where we will, some human hand has been
> Before us with its offering; not a tree
> Sprinkles these little pastures, but the same
> Hath furnished matter for a thought; perchance
> For some one serves as a familiar friend.

The fragment ends with the splendid Miltonic passage in which Wordsworth gives a visionary survey of his poetic intentions.

> Of Truth, of Grandeur, Beauty, Love and Hope,
> And melancholy Fear subdued by Faith;
> Of blessed consolations in distress;
> Of moral strength and intellectual power;
> Of joy in widest commonalty spread;
> Of the individual Mind that keeps her own
> Inviolate retirement, subject there
> To Conscience only, and the law supreme
> Of that Intelligence which governs all—
> I sing . . . .

> Paradise, and groves
> Elysian, Fortunate Fields—like those of old
> Sought in the Atlantic Main—why should they be
> A history only of departed things,
> Or a mere fiction of what never was?
> For the discerning intellect of Man,
> When wedded to this goodly Universe
> In love and holy passion, shall find these
> A simple produce of the common day.

Much of this ambition is fulfilled in the shorter poems of the years before 1807; and indeed the two passages above are hardly too grandiose a description of the best of Wordsworth's poetry. But according to the preface prefixed to *The Excursion* in 1814, these shorter poems were to be merely "the little cells, oratories and sepulchral recesses" attached to the great cathedral of which *The Prelude* was to be the antechapel. We must turn then to the only part of the great cathedral that was built—to *The Excursion*—to trace the progress of this splendid scheme.

But let us first remark that some of the little oratories are in a different style from the rest of the edifice. *The Song at the Feast of Brougham Castle* and *The White Doe of Rylstone* are wide departures from the usual Wordsworthian plan. They take us into the age of chivalry; and they are fictions, not the direct commerce of the heart with "substantial things". Yet both subdue the externals of romance to an essentially Words-worthian purpose. *Brougham Castle* is based on the story of Lord Clifford, dispossessed in infancy and brought up by shepherds, at last restored to his estates. The minstrel's song in which this is celebrated is in vigorous octosyllabics, owing something to Gray and something to Scott; but the essence of the poem is in the closing lines, spoken in the poet's own person. The minstrel is simply hailing the return of a feudal lord: but Lord Clifford's experiences among the shepherds have brought a development of his nature that his subjects do not suspect.

> Love had he found in huts where poor men lie;
> His daily teachers had been woods and rills;
> The silence that is in the starry sky,
> The sleep that is among the lonely hills.

—lines which might as well have come from the *Leech-Gatherer* or *Michael* as from a poem on a chivalric theme.

The beautiful and perhaps rather neglected poem, *The White Doe of Rylstone*, is Wordsworth's only attempt at a sustained romantic narrative. He tells us in a note that it had been thoughtlessly compared to Scott's metrical romances, but he is himself perfectly clear about the difference.

Scott deals with adventure and external turns of fortune, and confines himself to that sphere. But "everything that is attempted by the principal persons in *The White Doe* fails, so far as its object is external and substantial. So far as it is moral and spiritual it succeeds". The tale is apparently one of adventure and conflict. But the hero refuses to take sides, follows his father and brothers in their revolt, but goes unarmed and is determined not to fight. When their cause is lost, the heroine, his sister, finds her comfort and exaltation in following her brother's injunction "not to interfere with the current of events, either to forward or delay them". The doe who becomes her companion seems to be a natural symbol of the spirit of contemplation in which she ends her life. This is one of Wordsworth's very few attempts at embodying his conceptions in a deliberately devised mythological form. It is characteristic that he should use his nearest approach to a story of action to enforce his most quietist lesson.

The Excursion appeared in 1814; but being a part of the plan that occupied Wordsworth's mind for a great part of his life, it was not all composed at one time. Some of it is very early; the story of Margaret in Book I was partly written before 1795: it is therefore the predecessor of *Michael* and the other blank verse idylls. Book IV, lines 1207–1274 were written by 1798: Books II and III, with the rest of IV were planned and partly written in 1806. The remainder dates from 1811–14.[17] For the most part, then, *The Excursion* belongs to Wordsworth's early middle-age, and it was subject to much revision throughout his life. Its discursive parts are in externals similar to those of *The Prelude*—though now less personal. Wordsworth speaks not directly of the growth of his own mind, but through the mouths of assumed characters; and this is a loss of immediacy without any gain in dramatic force. He prefixed to *The Excursion* the closing lines of *The Recluse* fragment, beginning

On man, on nature, and on human life
Musing in solitude . . .

Musing on man is not the same thing as re-creating one's

experience; and the difference between reflection and energetic
creation is seen everywhere in the contrast between *The Excursion* and *The Prelude*. There are few passages in *The Excursion*
to compare with the moments of mystical exaltation, or the
glowing presentations of physical joy in the early books of *The
Prelude*. The best part of Wordsworth's mind is the concrete
part—the part that deals with immediate experience. In *The
Prelude* that is what he is doing—retracing an actual course
of development. In *The Excursion* he is excogitating an argument; his scheme is not given, it is constructed; and not only
is the construction weak, but the organic weakness communicates itself to the style, and there is much flatness and
diffusion. It is over the reading of *The Excursion* that the
professed Wordsworthian and the unpartisan reader of poetry
are most likely to part company.

What has happened to bring about the change? Failure of
impulse, or the abnegation of his deepest-rooted convictions in
favour of a conventionally conservative middle age, are the
common explanations. Probably Wordsworth has explained it
best himself—in the *Immortality Ode* and, more clearly, in the
Ode to Duty. This dates from 1805; but it already contains
within it the germs of Wordsworth's middle age. The poem
first proclaims the happiness of those who act rightly from an
instinctive joy and confidence:

> There are who ask not if thine eye
> Be on them; who in love and truth,
> Where no misgiving is, rely
> Upon the genial sense of youth.
> Glad hearts! Without reproach or blot
> Who do thy work, and know it not.

But when this happy self-trust begins to fail, the power of
duty must be called in to supply its place. The sense of something
lost is as clear as in the *Immortality Ode* (or, for that matter, in
Tintern Abbey): and the poem ends with the same assertion that
something else can be found which will be abundant recom-

pense for what has gone. There is no reason to doubt that
Wordsworth was perfectly sincere in this. He did achieve a
serenity and control in his middle years that was not achieved
by any other of the romantic poets, and morally this is admirable: but unhappily what has been lost was what produced the
poetry; and this Wordsworth never clearly saw. He hails with
perfect genuineness a gain in conscious purpose; but as his
earlier writing constantly tells us, he was not a poet in whom
conscious purpose did the essential work. In *The Excursion* he
is not one of those "who do thy work and know it not": he
knows only too well what he is doing. He is expounding a
personal philosophy of which he is clearly aware in advance;
and his best poetry comes when something of which he is not
yet clearly aware expresses itself through him.

But it is not a negligible philosophy. One who is in sympathy with the Wordsworthian ethos can read *The Excursion*
with edification and a temperate pleasure: anyone who wishes
to understand the nineteenth century must read it. It is one of
the great reassertions of traditional values against the unhistorical rationalist optimism of the enlightenment. The principal
characters are the Wanderer, one of Wordsworth's philosophers
from humble life—a leech-gatherer grown improbably articulate
and self-conscious; and the Solitary, one who has given himself
to revolutionary hopes, suffered the inevitable disillusion, and
has never found anything to take the place of what he now
thinks to have been the false idealism of his youth. The purpose
of the argument is to combat the Solitary's misanthropy and
morbid isolation and bring him back to juster views. In this the
Wanderer is abetted by the Pastor, who supplements the
Wanderer's natural religion by urging the claims of revelation
and a church establishment. Interspersed are many anecdotes,
accounts of rural lives, in the familiar Wordsworthian vein, but
rarely with much of the old inspiration. One would rather have
them in the prose of Dorothy's journals than in this unpoetical
poetry. The Wanderer's faith is that which we have already
seen Wordsworth working out for himself—in *The Prelude*,
Tintern Abbey and the fragment of *The Recluse*. And this, perhaps, is the key to the lack of poetical *élan* in *The Excursion*—

Wordsworth is expounding a philosophy which he is by now in possession of, fully formed: the poetry came in the process of forming it. But all the questions are now settled, and the Wanderer knows all the answers; and the Solitary's disillusions and despairs are only ninepins set up to be bowled over:

> as no cause
> Could e'er for such exalted confidence
> Exist; so, none is now for fixed despair:
> The two extremes are equally disowned
> By reason: if with sharp recoil, from one
> You have been driven far as its opposite,
> Between them seek the point to build
> Sound expectation.

—lines in which recollections of the eighteenth century and the coming Victorian *via media* are curiously mingled. Bits of the eighteenth century get rather oddly into the verse, too; indeed Wordsworth henceforth often seems to forget his earlier campaign against "poetic diction".

> What other spirit can it be that prompts
> The gilded summer flies to mix and weave
> Their sports together in the solar beam,
> Or in the gloom of twilight hum their joy?
> More obviously the self-same influence rules
> The feathered kinds.

But the direction of the poem is towards the Victorian age: if it were more read, it would go far to reduce the supposition of a sharp break between the earlier romantic generation and those who began to write after 1830. The familiar Victorian problems begin to make their appearance—the growth of industrialism and its consequences, popular education; and the desire to find answers that will combine the possibility of progress with an emotional traditionalism. Especially typical is the process by which, after the magnificent entry of the Wanderer's natural religion, serenely deduced from universal experience, the whole of Anglican theology and church government is smuggled in behind it, and is found to fit so well into the landscape that it remains without any further examination of its credentials.

Indeed, *The Excursion* is a justification, in the light of Wordsworth's own experience, of traditional ways of life, of traditional morals and traditional pieties. It assumes that the essential conditions in which human nature will find its satisfaction are already known, and that they will not change. To that extent it is unprogressive, and quite different from the faith with which the young Wordsworth had beheld human nature seeming born again. But Wordsworth's later Toryism is not mainly political: it results from the need to find his intuitions embodied in institutions and in a way of life. A mystical experience inspired by the contemplation of Nature was at the heart of his sensibility: but man cannot live by nature-mysticism alone, and Wordsworth is seeking in *The Excursion* a pattern of human life in which his natural religion can find its proper setting.

Beyond *The Excursion* we need hardly follow him. At this point his ideas were formed and settled. His best poetry had been a product of their development: now that the development is complete the poetry almost stops. Wordsworth wrote a great many verses after 1815, and was to live for forty years more, a serene and well-organized existence: but apart from some repetition of earlier lyric themes, and occasional fine sonnets, there is nothing in the remainder of his work that we could not well spare.

By unregenerate radicals who had kept their earlier political ideals raw and untempered this was seen as Nemesis overtaking the poet for treachery to his revolutionary past; and the "Lost Leader" tradition persisted into the next age, as we can see in Browning's poem. Did not Wordsworth accept the patronage of Lord Lonsdale and Sir George Beaumont, and, ultimately, a Crown sinecure? He did indeed: but the lines

> Just for a handful of silver he left us
> Just for a riband to stick in his coat

become quite absurd when we recall that Wordsworth had forsaken revolutionary liberalism years before he became Distributor of Stamps for the county of Westmorland. Both Wordsworth and Coleridge were more deferential to Sir George Beaumont than was altogether appropriate, but there is no ground for the supposition that they had sold themselves to the ruling class. The case of Coleridge is indeed different. He achieved none of Wordsworth's semi-official status; he spent a philosophic old age, of social obscurity but astonishing intellectual influence; and his later views were so original, and so far from conventional Toryism, that it would be fantastic to suggest that he developed into a complacent supporter of the *status quo*.

There is no more to record of Coleridge's poetical history. In 1816, after a period of miserable disintegration, he found refuge in the household of the kindly Dr. Gillman at Highgate, thought of finishing *Christabel*, but never did; and developed into the Table-Talker, the thinker aloud. Yet it was in this period that he had his greatest effect on the thought of his time, and it was the works of this period, *Aids to Reflection* (1825), *On the Constitution of Church and State* (1840), and *The Confessions of an Enquiring Spirit* (posthumously published, 1840), that were to exercise such an immense influence on the young intellectuals of the rising Victorian generation. Coleridge's influence is very fully recorded in John Stuart Mill's essay;[18] but its extent is still, perhaps, not generally realized, and we must find room for a word on his later ideas.

In general, he was moving in the same direction as Wordsworth, but independently, for there was little intercourse between them after 1810. Like Wordsworth, he passed from an indefinite uninstitutional religion to a firm support of the Anglican establishment; and to a respect for something like the traditional hierarchy of English society, or rather, a sort of Platonic idea of English society. But his reaction from revolutionary radicalism was both more violent and more intellectual than Wordsworth's, and instead of finding an alternative in an established pattern of life, he sought it in German idealist philosophy. The vexed question of his relation with the German transcendentalists cannot concern us here; what is important is that he evolved, whether from this source, or from his own inner consciousness, a type of religious apologetic that was to form the staple of Victorian broad-church thought, and was not without its influence even on the Oxford movement. It is a thorough-going subjectivism: Christianity is defended, not by external proofs, but by its correspondence with the needs of the human heart.

"*Evidences* of Christianity! I am weary of the word. Make a man feel the *want* of it; rouse him to the *need* of it; and you may safely trust it to its own *evidence*."

This passage, from the conclusion of *Aids to Reflection* points clearly enough to *In Memoriam*, where the ultimate answer to religious difficulties is "The heart stood up and answered 'I have felt'." Among Coleridge's Highgate disciples were F. D. Maurice, John Sterling and Julius Hare, all leading lights of Tennysonian Cambridge; so the influence was probably direct enough. In *The Confessions of an Enquiring Spirit* is a proposal for a more liberal interpretation of Scripture: and when, in years to come, evolutionary theory and the higher criticism came to threaten the Christian position, its defenders found in Coleridge's work weapons ready to their hand.

Socially, Coleridge's thought is equally remarkable. In *The Constitution of Church and State*, he carries on the work of Burke in opposing, to Jacobin theories of equality and natural rights, the notion of society as an organism—not a Marxian battle ground of conflicting class interests, or a Godwinian concourse of individualisms, but an interrelated whole, whose parts only have meaning in relation to the whole. In this conception, the Church, as the organized expression of the nation's learning and piety, plays an important part: and it is worth noting that both Wordsworth and Coleridge, apart from any devotional sentiment, conceived a perfectly clear *political* admiration for the Church as a national institution. In his consciousness of the threat to traditional values of the Benthamite ideology of the new manufacturers, Coleridge resembles the Wordsworth of *The*

Excursion: and both look forward to the Carlyle of *Past and Present* and the Ruskin of *Unto This Last*. The common picture of Coleridge as wasting into deliquescence after a few brief flashes of poetical greatness is quite untrue. Though it is outside our field, it should be recorded here that recent work on Coleridge has all tended to re-emphasize his philosophical importance; a closer study of Victorian letters must continue to reveal his dominant influence in later nineteenth-century thought—and how mistaken is the patronage sometimes bestowed on his supposedly wasted powers.

NOTES

Chapter II.   Wordsworth and Coleridge

1. I owe most of what is said in these paragraphs to Basil Willey, *The Seventeenth Century Background* and *The Eighteenth Century Background*. The latter especially should be consulted for the development of the idea of Nature.

2. References to *The Prelude* are to the 1805 version.

3. In Brailsford, *Shelley, Godwin and their Circle*; and in Harper, *William Wordsworth*, I, 253-260.

4. This was not Coleridge's view; he already thought Wordsworth the first poet of the age; and it is true that the story of Margaret in *Excursion*, Book I had already been begun. Wordsworth had thus begun to develop his austere blank-verse manner before meeting Coleridge.

5. *Biog. Lit.*, Chap. XIV.

6. *v.* Lionel Trilling, "The Immortality Ode", in *The Liberal Imagination*, 1951.

7. *v.* the essay "Wordsworth in the Tropics", in *Do What You Will*.

8. He designedly omits speculations of this kind: *v. Road to Xanadu*, note, p. 400.

9. *v.* Fenwick note to "We are Seven".

10. Coleridge, *Table-Talk*, May 31, 1830.

11. It is discussed from this point of view in Maud Bodkin, *Archetypal Patterns in Poetry*. For other studies of A. M. *v.* G. Wilson Knight, *The Starlit Dome*, 1941; and E. M. W. Tillyard, *Five Poems*, 1948. (Re-issued as *Poetry and its Background*, 1955.)

12. But this has been doubted. On this, and K. K. in general *v.* E. Schneider *The Dream of Kubla Khan*. Publication of Modern Language Association of America, 1945.

13. In *The Decline and Fall of the Romantic Ideal*.

14. *Biog. Lit.*, ed. Shawcross. See the detailed and learned introduction.

Also I. A. Richards, *Coleridge on Imagination* (1934), where Coleridge's doctrines are discussed from a very un-Coleridgean philosophical standpoint; and D. G. James, *Scepticism and Poetry*, 1937, where Richards's views are criticized.

15. *v.* Raysor, *Coleridge's Shakespearean Criticism*, I, 213; and Richards, *op. cit.*

16. *v. Works*, ed. de Selincourt, V, 475.

17. ibid. V, 369-72.

18. In *Dissertations and Discussions*; also *Mill on Bentham and Coleridge*, ed. F. R. Leavis.

CHAPTER III

BYRON

WITHIN the lifetime of Wordsworth and Coleridge a new generation of poets, linked by their fortunes, and to some extent by their poetic ideals, was to grow up, to write and to die. Yet Byron, Shelley and Keats do form a distinct generation, and mark a new phase of the English poetic tradition, for their work did not begin to appear until the great period of their predecessors was past. Byron was the eldest of them, and his juvenile poems came out in 1807, the year which we usually take to mark the beginning of Wordsworth's poetic decline. Only ten years after the Wordsworthian dawn, indeed; but already the historical picture was looking very different. Byron and his contemporaries were too young ever to have seen the revolution in its pristine glory; they had never seen France standing on the top of golden hours and human nature seeming born again; they grew up into a world in which England seemed to be permanently at war with France, in which the reaction against revolutionary ideals was in full swing; and their early maturity saw political reaction victorious all over Europe. All were liberals, Byron and Shelley by conviction, Keats mainly by association; and they lived in a world where liberals were generally on the defensive and not infrequently in prison. Wordsworth and Coleridge had taken part in a great movement of the spirit at a time when all the forces of nature seemed to be on its side. The possibility that their way of life might coincide with the way the world was going was, therefore, perfectly real to them. Their long search for balance and order seemed a possible quest; indeed, in the end it succeeded, though in a region far removed from that of their original expectations. To the poets who grew up to the Europe of Castlereagh and Metternich opposition seemed the inevitable attitude; revolt, both social and personal, for Byron and Shelley; mere non-co-operation for Keats. Thus, curiously enough, it is the older men,

Wordsworth and Coleridge, whose work leads naturally into the next age—*The Excursion* and *Aids to Reflection* are footpaths to the cultivated Victorian countryside—while their juniors die unreconciled in the romantic solitudes of their choice.

Byron is the most difficult of all the nineteenth-century poets to write about in purely critical terms. As an influence and a portent he is, if we take the European scene as a whole, by far the most powerful. Yet much of the power is exercised in action and in self-dramatization rather than in art; the poetry seems to provide an insufficient foundation for the tremendous Byronic legend. In common opinion on the continent, he is still probably the greatest English poet after Shakespeare: personality is a more easily exportable product than poetry, perhaps more readily disposable even than ideas. "As soon as he reflects, he is a child", Goethe said of Byron: yet he is the one poet to whom Bertrand Russell devotes a chapter in the *History of Western Philosophy*. Thus if we are to do anything like justice to Byron as a historical phenomenon we can hardly treat him with the aesthetic detachment that modern criticism prefers. Modern criticism has, of course, been conscious of the dilemma; and it has found a way out by treating only that part of Byron's poetry that appeals to contemporary taste. Yet that will hardly do either—for it was not by that part of his work that Byron's reputation was chiefly made. Here we shall compromise, and try to do what justice we can to both the "historic" and the "real" estimate of Byron. With the Byron legend we can hardly deal: it has been fed not only by his own work, but by a mass of gossip, memoir and biography; and we can only refer the reader to a brief list of sources. Historical scholarship and romantic evocation have both had their way with Byron; and an abbreviated sketch of his life would have no chance of revealing the lasting fascination of his personality.

The outline of the story is well enough known: his ancestry —his father a disreputable rake who married a Scottish heiress for her money, and died, leaving her poor to bring up a lame boy in Aberdeen: his childhood, passed in narrow circumstances, with a vulgar and violent mother: and then the sudden inheritance which made him, at ten years old, Lord Byron, and

master of Newstead. He embraced his new dignities with an
un-English and unaristocratic passion. Harrow introduced him
to the world of young men of his class, and he threw himself
into it with fiery energy; but remained always moody, aloof,
dangerously handsome, and unassimilated to ordinary society.
His passion went into boyish friendships, and later into boyish
loves. His first volume of poems appeared when he was still at
Cambridge—appropriately named *Hours of Idleness*; neither
better nor worse than many another young man's poetry. Why
it should have been selected for attack by the *Edinburgh Review*
is hard to see, except that its author was a lord. Perhaps the
eagle eye of the Scottish critic detected within this modest
volume the embryo of the daemonic figure that was to come.
At all events, Byron was deeply outraged by the *Edinburgh*
critique, and after some meditation, produced his first good
poem in reply.

English Bards and Scotch Reviewers is a satire, going back
ultimately to the *Dunciad* for inspiration, but mediated by
William Gifford's crude and hard-hitting *Baviad* and *Maeviad*.
Morally and critically there is not much to be said for a poem
whose inspiration was little more than bad temper, and Byron
was later ashamed of it. It lashes out indiscriminately at the
whole literary world of the time, and has none of the finesse of
Popian satire. The worst of writing a satire in heroic couplets is
that the genre has been carried as far as it can go by Pope: and
Byron adds nothing to the tradition except the impress of a
new personality—a certain careless arrogance that was to be
the note of so much of his best work. The pretence of
lofty concern for intellectual standards sits ill on him, but
characteristically he gives an impish denial of the claims of
criticism in almost the same breath.

> A man must serve his time to every trade
> Save censure—critics all are ready made.
> Take hackneyed jokes from Miller, learned by rote,
> With just enough of learning to misquote . . .
> . . . Care not for feeling, pass your proper jest,
> And stand a Critic, hated yet caressed.   (68)

Byron adopts the rôle of a defender of eighteenth-century intelligence and propriety against romantic extravagance. Scott, Wordsworth, Coleridge and Southey all come in for castigation, often amusing though rarely at all penetrating.

> Next comes the dull disciple of thy school,
> That mild apostate from poetic rule,
> The simple Wordsworth, framer of a lay
> As soft as evening in his favourite May,
> Who warns his friend to "shake off toil and trouble,
> And quit his books, for fear of growing double;"
> Who both by precept and example shows
> That prose is verse and verse is merely prose.
>
> (235)

It is significant, however, of the difference between Byron and his contemporaries that his first success should be in the use of the negative emotions of irritation and contempt.

The opportunity for constructing the more positive Byronic *persona* arose through travel. In 1809 Byron and his friend Hobhouse set out on a journey, at first through Spain and Portugal, and ultimately to Albania and Greece. The result of this was the first two cantos of *Childe Harold's Pilgrimage*. The conception of this poem is extremely mixed. In part it is a sort of verse-Baedeker, with historical and geographical reflections on the places visited. Spain and Portugal were of course familiar to Englishmen from the recent Peninsular campaign; and this provides a good deal of the background of the first canto. Greece was much less known, though Oriental travel books were popular; and here Byron was able to draw both on memories of the heroic past and on the attractions of the contemporary exotic. Both cantos are tinctured with a rather superficial liberalism, with the exhortations of which Englishmen used to be fond (the taste has now passed to America) to the degenerate Greeks and Spaniards to arise and remember their former virtue. All this is more objective and outward looking than Romantic poetry has been hitherto. But the poem has two legs to stand on—the historical and topographical material being

one, the other being the character of the hero. Childe Harold
is the first appearance of the Byronic hero. In the MS. the name
was first written Childe Burun (an old form of Byron), so that
an identification between hero and author was obvious. Byron
later obscured it by altering the names and uttering denials.
But it is clear enough that Childe Harold is simply the first of
many fancy portraits of himself. All the features that are soon
to become so familiar—the fatal ancestry, the excesses, the
satiety—are celebrated in the first few stanzas; and most characteristic of all, the collocation of gloomy debauchery with an
ideal of purity once glimpsed but now unattainable and
abandoned.

> For he through sin's long labyrinth had run,
> Nor made atonement when he did amiss,
> Had sighed to many though he loved but one,
> And that loved one, alas! could ne'er be his.
> Ah, happy she! to 'scape from him whose kiss
> Had been pollution unto aught so chaste;
> Who soon had left her charms for vulgar bliss
> And spoiled her goodly lands to gild his waste,
> Nor calm domestic peace had ever deigned to taste.
>
> **(I, v)**

This kind of hero has, of course, his literary ancestors.[1] The
pride and evil go back to Milton's Satan, the gloom and the
peculiar relation to women to some of the heroes of the novel of
terror. But the specially Byronic contribution is the interweav-
ing into the fictitious image of a number of more or less personal details, so that a shifting, but ever-present relationship
between self-portraiture and fantasy is set up. It was this
romantic self-portraiture that was to have such an extensive
effect on the romanticism of the continent. By its means Byron
is enabled to exploit his personality to the full, without being
tied within the limits of the authentic confession.

It must be confessed that the verse is not very distinguished.
The Spenserian stanza requires some approach to the Spenserian richness and dreamy music. Byron's conventional

vocabulary and on the whole commonplace rhythm seem to
vulgarize it—just as the slapdash methods of *English Bards* vulgarize the heroic couplet. Byron has not yet found the medium
that was to suit him best. But as usual with him, the total effect
is better than analysis of the details would suggest. A half-
hearted attempt at Spenserian archaism is soon forgotten after
the opening stanzas; and the topographical descriptions are
vigorous and interesting. It is, after all, a merit in poetry not to
be boring, and Byron is extremely skilful at varying his scenes
and subject-matter. The squalor of Lisbon is quickly followed
by a Salvatoresque picture of Cintra; Beckford is recalled, who
once lived there—with perhaps a side-glance at the parallel
between his temperament and Byron's own; we pass to contemporary politics—to a bitter denunciation of the Convention
of Cintra; and return to the melancholy and restlessness of the
Childe's state of mind. And all this in the space of twelve
stanzas (I, XVI–XXVII). Unlike some other exploiters of a
temperament, Byron does not make the mistake of giving it
insufficient food. Scenery, politics, history and manners, with a
little love-making, give Childe Harold plenty to occupy his mind.
Even at this unformed stage of his career Byron has a more
observant eye for the general spectacle of the world than any of
his contemporaries; and it is the world as seen through a dis-
tinctly realized temperament—not a mere guide-book catalogue.
Questions of the "sincerity" of Byron's portrayal of his hero are
irrelevant—he is a *persona*, a mask from which the poet can
effectively speak.

The second canto, about Greece and Albania, has the
advantage of novel scenes and manners; but more important is
Byron's passionate feeling for Greece. Greece was to see the
beginning, as it was to see the end, of his active life. His love
for the country and its people was compounded of many
elements; the love for the classical past—which has been felt
as strongly by idle as by industrious schoolboys; the love that
men who travel much often experience for the first place in
which they sojourn, the place that compounds itself with their
own undimmed sense of youth and adventure; the real strangeness and adventurousness of Greek and Moslem life; and the

excitement of political liberalism, which was already beginning
to stir on behalf of the Greeks against their Turkish overlords.
More even than Spain, Greece arouses the pathos of the past,
of fallen grandeur (II. I–IX); this fuses naturally with one of
Byron's favourite topics of speculation—mortality, and even
immortality, if there is any:

> Yet if, as holiest men have deemed, there be
> A land of souls beyond that sable shore,
> To shame the doctrine of the Sadducee
> And sophist, madly vain of dubious lore;
> How sweet it were in concert to adore
> With those who made our mortal labours light!
>
> (II, viii)

And these thoughts in turn recall a mysterious Thou
> —whose Love and Life together fled,
> Have left me here to love and live in vain. (II, ix)

Thus Byron succeeds in mingling the ruins of the Parthenon
with his own being: and meanwhile Childe Harold is forgotten,
to be picked up again, after an excursus on the iniquitous
removal of the Elgin marbles, in stanza XVI, to continue his
topographical and amatory adventures. The last half of the
canto is a vivid description of Greek, Albanian and Turkish
manners: the journey ends at Marathon, which leads to a
lament for the decay of Greece (re-echoed in the famous 'Isles
of Greece' stanzas in *Don Juan*); then to a lament for mortality
in general, and at last a lament for the lost loved one of stanza
IX. So Europe and Hellas and history are spread out like a
panorama for the romantic temperament to brood over, and
weltschmerz, that real enough but somewhat vacuous emotion,
takes on a new fullness and variety.

Byron returned to England in 1811, and published these
two cantos of *Childe Harold* in 1812. By that time he was
frequenting the brilliant fashionable society of Whig London;
and the immediate success of the poem was partly due to the
rank and beauty and *panache* of its author. Byron was not the

man to lose such an opportunity. He rapidly followed up his success with a series of metrical romances—*The Giaour, The Bride of Abydos, The Corsair* and *Lara*—all appearing between 1812 and 1814. He always wrote rapidly, and was, besides, full of the affectation of "the gentleman who writes with ease". Much in the romances is little more than fashionable versification; but the fashion is one that Byron is setting himself. The first three are tales of love, crime and adventure in the near eastern lands which he had by now made his especial province; *Lara* is Gothic. There are a few memorable passages, notably the description of sunset at Athens in Canto III of *The Corsair*; but this was written on the spot and transferred to its present place as an afterthought. For the most part in the tales Byron is employing the Scott formula for tales in verse, but adding a sombre element of mystery and evil which makes it a far more potent brew. He is also developing the character of the Byronic hero[1]—the dark, beautiful, blighted being who was inevitably to become more and more closely identified with himself, till his own actual career seems forced by some inner compulsion to follow the lines sketched out for it in fiction. Many men exploit their fantasies, but those who carry the process as far as Byron did are apt to find that the fantasies exact their revenge, and either enforce a growing isolation from the real world, or, as in Byron's case, force their way into the world and begin to enact themselves in reality.

Byron's fashionable career was attended with a number of picturesque love-affairs, on various emotional levels, the most famous being with Lady Caroline Lamb, whose egotism, vanity and theatrical sense were quite a match for his own. He tries hard to adopt the attitude of the Regency buck, sowing a tough crop of wild oats: but his case is really different. He is not playing the game for the fun of it; he is satisfying some obscurer impulse. The affectation of mysterious wickedness had begun when he was little more than a boy; and now he is doing his best to make it true. He wants to feel guilty; and the contrast between debauchery and an ideal purity, so frequent in the poetry, becomes a necessity to him. The ideal and sentimental side of his love-experiences (it is sentimental because it is pure fantasy, having no effects in action or in the discipline of the heart) appears in his lyrics; rather trivially in the famous *Maid of Athens*, more significantly in the sonnets to Genevra (Lady Frances Wedderburn Webster, a fragile and ethereal beauty for whom he cherished a passing tenderness), and in the group of poems to an unknown Thyrza, which seem to enshrine an idealized friendship with a Cambridge choir-boy. Conventionality of vocabulary and rhythm suggest something false and unrealized in these accessions of tenderness. Byron's verse was generally too slipshod and his emotions too large and untidy for the concentration that lyric requires; he never achieved either the loving absorption in the artistic process itself which produced Keats's *Odes*; or the complete identification of himself with the lyric mood that gave birth to some of Shelley's wisps of song. Byron stands aside, watching himself having feelings, and the lyrics become stucco garlands or paper rosettes, in curious contrast with the masculine straightforwardness he always shows in his letters. The letters show that he early acquired a sort of social assurance, and an ease and genuineness in equal friendships with men; but at this time at least, the poetry sprang from a less controllable part of his nature.

In 1815 he married a lady of rigid and uncompromising propriety. Byron seems to have treated her with consistent brutality, and the match broke up in the next year. It was rumoured that he had an incestuous love-affair with his half-sister (a report that later evidence has fully confirmed).[2] the whole thing blew up into one of the scandals in high-life so beloved of British society: Byron was ostracized by the people who had idolized him: and he left England in 1816, never to return.

He travelled through the Low Countries and up the Rhine, eventually to Geneva where he was soon joined by the Shelleys who had left England under a similar necessity. These German and Italian travels produced the third canto of *Childe Harold*. The formula seems at first sight the same as before—musings on the field of Waterloo, Alpine and Rhineland scenery, reminiscences of Rousseau, Gibbon and Voltaire: but there is actually a change of spirit. The distinction between the Childe and his

creater is now virtually abandoned; and the author-hero has no
need of factitious sorrows: he has enough real ones. The opening stanzas give an idea of Byron's state of mind on leaving
England, and give, too, a statement of the system of objectified
egotism on which his poetic practice is based.

> 'Tis to create, and in creating, live
> A being more intense that we endow
> With form our fancy, gaining as we give
> The life we image, even as I do now—
> What am I? Nothing: but not so art thou,
> Soul of my thought! With whom I traverse earth
> Invisible but gazing, as I glow
> Mixed with thy spirit, blended with thy birth,
> And feeling still with thee in my crushed feelings'
>   dearth.
>
> (III, vi)

Art is to subserve the ends of life and experience. Byron
could never have understood Mr. Eliot's distinction between
the man who suffers and the poet who creates. He writes as an
expansion of his personal being: and where man and society have
failed him, he now projects his feelings into the natural world.

> Where rose the mountains, there to him were friends;
> Where rolled the Ocean, thereon was his home;
> Where a blue sky, and glowing clime, extends,
> He had the passion and the power to roam;
> The desert, forest, cavern, breaker's foam,
> Were unto him companionship; they spake
> A mutual language, clearer than the tone
> Of his land's tongue, which he would oft forsake
> For Nature's pages glassed by sunbeams on the lake.
>
> (III, xiii)

Byron does not look to Nature to find in it some spiritual
essence that is actually there; he looks to it to echo and include
his own passions. Occasionally these are idyllic, as in the stanzas

on Clarens (XCIX–CIV), a landscape dedicated to love, because Rousseau made it the scene of the *Nouvelle Heloise*. More often they are tumultuous, as in the description of an Alpine thunderstorm that immediately precedes.

> Sky—Mountains—River—Winds—Lake—Lightnings! ye!
> With night, and clouds, and thunder—and a Soul
> To make these felt and feeling, well may be
> Things that have made me watchful; the far roll
> Of your departing voices, is the knoll
> Of what in me is sleepless,—if I rest.
> But where of ye, O Tempests! is the goal?
> Are ye like those within the human breast?
> Or do ye find, at length, like eagles, some high nest?
>
> Could I embody and unbosom now
> That which is most within me,—could I wreak
> My thoughts upon expression, and thus throw
> Soul—heart—mind—passions—feelings—strong or weak
> All that I would have sought, and all I seek,
> Bear, know, feel—and yet breathe—into *one* word,
> And that one word were Lightning, I would speak;
> But as it is, I live and die unheard,
> With a most voiceless thought, sheathing it as a sword.
>
> (III, xcvi, xcvii)

The verse hardly repays examination in details; there is crudity and incoherence, and little distinction in individual images: yet the energy of self-assertion in such lines was to alter the emotional scenery of Europe; to the sorrows and the sentiment of Werther, the lubricities and tenderness of Rousseau's *Confessions*, has been added a stormy vigour without which the Romantic picture of the heart's landscape would be incomplete. In the closing stanzas of this canto Byron finds a new assurance, the tone of "a man speaking to men", which he was to use to still better purpose, mockingly or seriously, in verses yet to come.

I have not loved the World, nor the World me,
But let us part fair foes; I do believe,
Though I have found them not, that there may be
Words which are things—hopes which will not deceive
And Virtues which are merciful, nor weave
Snares for the failing: I would also deem
O'er others' griefs that some sincerely grieve—
That two, or one, are almost what they seem,
That Goodness is no name—and Happiness no dream.
                                        (III, cxiv)

The fourth canto is more historical in purport; Dante, Petrarch, Tasso, Venice and the ruins of Rome are its themes; but its central subject is Italy, the longest of Byron's loves among the nations, as Greece was the first and the last: and Italy seen as a symbol of all human achievement in arts and arms, its splendour and decay. For all his egoism, Byron is more conscious of Europe, of history, of the march of human destiny, than any of his contemporaries. For this reason he must be read *in extenso*. His large subjects and his loose style do not fit into snippets, and the present fashion for minute analysis of short passages, and for divorcing poetry from its historic context can hardly do it justice. A more leisured and less meticulous view of poetry would do much to restore *Childe Harold*'s former lustre; and the poem is, in any case, the indispensable prologue to the later satires.

Manfred belongs to the same period as Canto III of *Childe Harold*. The hero is the familiar Satanic figure; and the sense of guilt and the hint of an incestuous love embody the moods of Byron's first months after leaving England. Its dramatic but untheatrical form and its visionary nature are the result of a reading of Goethe's *Faust*; but the impression of *Faust* on such an unmetaphysical nature as Byron's was not likely to be very profound. The best comment on *Manfred* is Byron's own:

"I forgot to mention to you that a kind of Poem in dialogue (in blank verse) or drama . . . is finished; it is in three acts; but of a very wild, metaphysical, and inexplicable kind.

Almost all the persons—but two or three—are spirits of the earth and air, or the waters; the scene is in the Alps; the hero is a kind of magician, who is tormented by a species of re-morse, the cause of which is left half unexplained. He wanders about invoking these spirits, which appear to him, and are of no use; he at last goes to the very abode of the Evil principle *in propria persona*, to evocate a ghost, which appears, and gives him an ambiguous and disagreeable answer; and in the 3rd act he is found by his attendants dying in a tower where he studies his art. You may perceive by this outline that I have no great opinion of this piece of fantasy."[1]

Except as a document in Byronic psychology we may per-haps be excused from having any great opinion of it either.

After the completion of Canto III of *Childe Harold*, Byron went to Venice. He was in a savage and desperate mood, and solaced himself with a kind of bitter debauchery brilliantly described in letters to Moore and Murray. The contrast already remarked between the intimate and half-unconscious self-revelation of the poetry and the more critical and worldy tone of the letters is curiously brought out by his comment on this canto:

"I tremble for the magnificence which you attribute to the new *Childe Harold*. I am glad you like it; it is a fine in-distinct piece of poetical desolation, and my favourite. I was half-mad during the time of its composition, between meta-physics, mountains, lakes, love unextinguishable, thoughts unutterable, and the nightmare of my own delinquencies. I should, many a good day, have blown my brains out, but for the recollection that it would have given pleasure to my mother-in-law."[2]

The man who suffers and the poet who creates had been the same; here we have another man standing aside and mocking at both. The tone of these two extracts suggests a more or less deliberate denial of the mood in which *Manfred* and the new

Childe Harold were written. The best of Byron's short lyrics also belongs to this time.

> So we'll go no more a-roving
> So late into the night
> Though the heart be still as loving
> And the moon be still as bright.

Written in a Lenten interval between excesses,[3] it is also a sad little farewell to the lyric and idyllic hopes that had thrown an intermittent light on Byron's youth. From now on, the Byron of the letters begins to extend his operations into poetry. His savage mood passed; he moderated his debaucheries, and began a more temperate course of social pleasure. And he began to find that he was enjoying himself. He was sick of ardours and despairs, the easy-going tolerance of Venetian life delighted him; the man of the world began to gain upon the arrogant and feverish youth. The poetical result was *Beppo*, written in the autumn of 1817.

Byron had studied, among other Italian poetry, the mock-heroic versions of the Orlando cycle by Berni and Pulci, and wished to reproduce the gay impertinence of the style. There was an English model for this sort of thing in the *Whistlecraft*[4] poem of John Hookham Frere. In fact, the main thing that Byron takes from his models is the metre—the Italian *ottava rima*. For the first time he finds a medium that really suits him, and he is always far more at home in this stanza than in either couplets or the Spenserians of *Childe Harold*. The story of *Beppo* is of the slightest—a married woman's love affair, which instead of ending in the English fashion with a. duel, divorce and ostracism, settles down on the return of the husband into a comfortable *ménage à trois*. The leading theme is the contrast between English and Italian manners: but Byron is discovering something more than a metre and a social mode that suit him: he is discovering his own maturity—a tolerant *mariage de convenance* between his temperament and the world as it is. The stanza, with its concluding couplet, often used for an impertinent or epigrammatic final twist or a sudden unexpected bathos, is suited to the casual, digressive manner. The looseness and slackness of his verse is now turned into a merit, a positive ingredient of his style, not an accidental defect. The apparent flippancy is often more serious than earlier rhetorical transports, just as the familiar letters are often more serious than the soulful lyrics. Similarly the liaison with the Countess Guiccioli, begun in 1819 in the most frivolous Venetian spirit, proved to be indeed "the last attachment", and for all its vicissitudes, its periods of tedium, its occasional baseness, to be more like a marriage than anything else that Byron ever knew.

Beppo, of course, is not the whole story. It represents the formation, the settlement of a part of Byron's personality: but the turbid aspirations of *Childe Harold* were not so easily quenched. Part of these found their way into the unliterary activities of his last years, part into the tragedies and "mysteries", part into *Don Juan*. *Don Juan* was begun in the autumn of 1818, shortly after the composition of *Beppo*, and in much the same spirit. Indeed *Beppo* could well have formed an episode in the longer poem. But *Don Juan* was to prove a very long poem—the first five cantos were written at intervals between 1818 and 1820, the remaining eleven between 1822 and 1823; and a fragment of a seventeenth turned up among Byron's papers in Greece at the time of his death. It thus occupied him for the last five years of his life, though not exclusively; for apart from the demands of politics and the Countess Guiccioli he had a period of astonishing productivity in 1820-2. But the best of his experience went into *Don Juan*. He wrote to Moore in September 1818, "I have finished the first canto . . . of a poem in the style and manner of *Beppo* . . . It is called *Don Juan*, and is meant to be a little quietly facetious upon everything. But I doubt whether it is not—at least as far as it has yet gone—too free for these very modest days." The initial intention, then, is a poem of a light, social-satiric kind; but there is the possibility of its developing in other directions. In the end, the poem turns out to be most remarkable for its extent and its variety. By abandoning the Satanic-Promethean pose of the early poems, Byron has given himself the advantages of humour and ease and worldly wisdom: and from this relatively firm standpoint he can

survey with safety other aspects of experience, which hitherto
he has never been secure enough to deal with adequately.

An imposing array of literary sources can be made out for
Don Juan. Apart from his Italian originals, from which he
derived the metre, the free digressive manner, the indescribable
tone of mockery that does not exclude gravity and tenderness,
he owed much to the tradition of the picaresque novel. The
escapade which sends Juan on his travels, as well as some of his
later adventures, have their parallels in *Tom Jones*; the turn for
fantasy, digression and bawdiness remind us of Sterne. For a
story with such an immense variety of incident, told with such
picturesque detail, a great deal of concrete factual material was
required. Dalzell's *Shipwrecks and Disasters at Sea* provided
details of the shipwreck in Canto II; Castelnau's *Essai sur
l'histoire ancienne et moderne de la Nouvelle Russie* gave the
background of the siege of Ismail; various stray fragments of
romantic plot may have come from Dunlop's *History of Fiction*;
the atmosphere of the Haidee idyll seems to take some of its
colour from *Daphnis and Chloe*.[5] The outward-looking and
objective side of Byron's mind needed and was able to absorb a
good deal of matter, and his large desultory reading supplied it.
However, this does not explain the poem, any more than
Coleridge's reading of travel books explains the *Ancient
Mariner*. What gives it its direction is Byron's determination to
put into it as much as possible of his own experience of men, of
manners, of the way of the world, of his own heart, of the hearts
of women, undeterred by prudery or social restraints, inspired
by the kind of gay, disillusioned honesty that he had ultimately
achieved, after all his torments and affectations. Almost everything in the poem can be related to his own experience, though
it does not copy it. The recording of biographical parallels is
often trivial, and though, like any good poem, *Don Juan* can be
read without autobiographical reference, we can hardly understand its genesis without seeing, beside its panorama of European society, its fundamental subjective basis.

The scapegrace Juan of the first escapade is not Byron at
sixteen: but perhaps he is Byron as he would have liked to be—
Byron without the shyness, the lameness and the morbid pride.

Juan's straitlaced and mathematical mother preserves reminiscences, relatively unmalicious, of Lady Byron; and Donna Julia
represents the sort of amiably passionate and otherwise un-
exacting woman that Byron, of all the varieties of amatory
experience, had on the whole come to prefer. The tolerant,
mocking air is partly the fruit of his Venetian life, partly *pour
épater* the English and their commercial morality.

> Happy the nations of the moral North!
> Where all is virtue, and the winter season
> Sends sin without a rag on, shivering forth,
> ('Twas snow that brought St. Anthony to reason);
> Where juries cast up what a wife is worth
> By laying whate'er sum, in mulct, they please on
> The lover, who must pay a handsome price,
> Because it is a marketable vice.   (I, lxiv)

The gruesome realism of the shipwreck in Canto II, and the
vivid and horrible realism of the scenes at the siege of Ismail
(Cantos VII and VIII) are outside Byron's direct experience,
and rely heavily on literary sources; but he had after all seen
something of land travel and seafaring, something of adventure,
in his early journeyings in the Near East; there was much of
the man of action in him, and a physical adventurousness and
athleticism in which he is alone among his contemporaries. No
stay-at-home poet or merely ideal traveller could ever have
written these passages: nor could Byron's picture of the world
be complete without the recognition of violence, cruelty and
horror. Like any sane man, Byron hates them: but unlike many
nineteenth-century writers, he knows that they exist.

The exquisite Haidee episode (Cantos II, III and IV) is the
quintessence of all Byron's ideal longings, and of all his actual
experiences of idyllic love: the sentiment that has appeared so
fitfully in his earlier verse, so often submerged by Satanism
or sentimentalism, so totally irreconcilable in Byron's eyes with
the prudential realities of organized society. Yet for him it
remained real; and he makes it real, within the context of the
poem, by isolating it from all common ties. Juan appears from

the sea, unencumbered and anonymous, Haidee is alone and
responsible to none but her own heart; and their love is a
transitory idyll, without prelude and without sequel:

> —for they were children still
> And children still they should have ever been;
> They were not made in the real world to fill
> A busy character in the dull scene.   (IV, xv.)

It is Byron's simultaneous awareness of flat earthy reality
that makes the idyll possible. As soon as the real world, in the
shape of Haidee's father, returns—all is at an end; and so is
Haidee's life. If Byron had had the sense of an omnipresent
metaphysical background, he would have had to place the love
of Juan and Haidee somewhere in the scheme of things—subli-
mate it to a Platonic heaven, or consign it to a Dantean hell. If
he had continued it, and woven it into the texture of the rest of
life he would have had to show it changed and debased, according to his view of woman's actual lot:

> Alas, the love of Women! it is known
> To be a lovely and a fearful thing;
> For all of theirs upon that die is thrown,
> And if 'tis lost, Life hath no more to bring
> To them but mockeries of the past alone,
> And their revenge is as the tiger's spring
> Deadly, and quick, and crushing; yet as real
> Torture is theirs—what they inflict they feel.
>
> They are right, for Man, to man so oft unjust
> Is always so to women: one sole bond
> Awaits them—treachery is all their trust;
> Taught to conceal their bursting hearts despond
> Over their idol, till some wealthier lust
> Buys them in marriage—and what rests beyond?
> A thankless husband—next, a faithless lover—
> Then dressing, nursing, praying—and all's over.
>
> (II, cxcix,cc)

So Haidee dies: and Juan continues a career in which that
kind of love does not return: though there is a sexless attenuated
echo of it in his attachment to the waif Leila rescued from the
siege of Ismail.

In the English scenes the poem becomes even looser and
more digressive; and for its source turns again to personal
experience. The social life, the characters and the scenery are
those of the years of fame. Norman Abbey is modelled on
Newstead. The tone is satirical, the incidental reflections often
pungent, but the savagery of some of his earlier reflections on
England are gone. Byron retains his own scheme of values, and
it includes a pretty vigorous contempt for English society; but
there is a tolerance, even a half-affectionate reminiscence in this
backward look on a forsaken landscape. Just as the intrigue
seems to be under way the poem breaks off abruptly. The
demands of life—and death—superseded those of poetry.

Much ink has been spilt, both by contemporaries and later
critics, on the ethics of *Don Juan*. Byron meant to be shocking,
and he duly shocked: perhaps he did not realize how much the
social tone was changing in the twenties: Lady Blessington
remarked that he retained to the last the manners of the Regency
dandy, outmoded in England since he left it. But the poem
would not be what it is if it had been written merely *pour
épater*. However, the attempt to analyse its more serious intentions is not likely to be very successful: and it can safely be
said that whoever after reading it needs an exposition of its
motives is never likely to understand them. A few possible
misconceptions can be removed. The poem owes nothing to the
traditional Don Juan legend: it is not the story of a fatal and
heartless libertine. It is not, in the first place, Juan's story at
all; it is rather a picture of society—and Juan is there to show
the way the natural man might live in it. A natural man who was
luckier and simpler than Byron, who lived in action and in the
senses, untroubled by imagination or intelligence. For the
character of his hero Byron has cut out from his own character,
and consigned to oblivion, most of what went into the third
canto of *Childe Harold*, and left the social and amatory butterfly
that he sometimes aspired to be. But the hero is in the picaresque

tradition, a peg on which to hang the incidents: as a character
he is less important than the narrator, whose asides, comments,
descriptions and digressions give the story its indescribable
flavour. It is a commonplace to remark on the hatred of sham
and convention, the glorification of impulse and the natural
feelings in the poem; it should be noticed, too, how protean,
even contradictory, these natural feelings are; mockery of
prudishness and the calculating virtues, set against the purity
and candour of Haidee's love, the unanalysable affection between
Juan and Leila, even the queer, placid innocence of Dudu in the
harem; hatred of militarism and carnage set against an admiration for courage and action; scepticism and irreverence set
against the lovely lines on the Angelus.

> Ave Maria! blessed be the hour!
> The time, the clime, the spot, where I so oft
> Have felt that moment in its fullest power
> Sink o'er the earth—so beautiful and soft—
> While swung the deep bell in the distant tower,
> Or the faint dying day-hymn stole aloft,
> And not a breath crept through the rosy air,
> And yet the forest leaves seemed stirred with prayer.
>
> Ave Maria! 'tis the hour of prayer!
> Ave Maria! 'tis the hour of love!
> Ave Maria! may our spirits dare
> Look up to thine and to thy Son's above!
> Ave Maria! oh that face so fair!
> Those downcast eyes beneath the Almighty Dove—
> What though 'tis but a pictured image?—strike—
> That painting is no idol—'tis too like.   (III, cii, ciii)

None of these moods can stand alone: their meaning is in
their variety—even in their incongruity. The love of freedom is
built into the capricious structure of the poem; and *Don Juan*
justifies the romantic moral scheme, which is to reject all
formal schemes, in the only way that it can be justified—by
building up, out of impulses followed as they come, a personal

identity, an organic unity, that is possible in art, but that such a method could hardly achieve in life. If romantic art is, as some say, inherently more imperfect than classical, it is because it is less self-contained. Byron is using his art exactly as he says he uses it, to expand and complete his sense of his own being.

In 1820 Byron left Venice to follow the Countess Guiccioli to Ravenna. Her family were ardent Liberals, and Byron formed close relations with them, particularly with her younger brother, Count Pietro Gamba, an amiable and devoted figure who followed him to the last. There is little space here for a discussion of Byron's political convictions. Liberty was an essential part of the Byronic creed: but for him that ambiguous word often meant only the liberty for an anarchic and anti-social expression of the individual personality. By an easy extension, this passion for personal freedom comes to cover national freedom as well; and of course the chief political form of the struggle for freedom in that age was the struggle for national self-determination. Italy and Greece were the principal battle grounds for the post-Napoleonic age, and Byron identified himself with both of these emergent nationalisms. In Ravenna he became closely involved with that romantic and ineffectual secret society, the Carbonari. His diary of 1821 gives us an idea of their activities and his own part in them.

"I wonder what figure these Italians will make in a regular row. I sometimes think that, like the Irishman's gun (somebody had sold him a crooked one), they will only do for 'shooting round a corner'; at least that sort of shooting has been the late tenor of their exploits. And yet there are materials in these people, and a noble energy, if well-directed. But who is to direct them? No matter. Out of such times heroes spring. Difficulties are the hotbeds of high spirits, and Freedom the mother of the few virtues incident to human nature.[6]

They mean to *insurrect* here, and are to honour me with a call thereupon. I shall not fall back; though I don't think them in force or heart sufficient to make much of it. But, *onward!*—it is now the time to act, and what signifies *self*,

if a single spark of that which would be worthy of the past can
be bequeathed unquenchably to the future? It is not one man,
nor a million, but the *spirit* of liberty which must be spread.[7]

These are not the utterances of a facile or disengaged
sympathy, and all the evidence seems to show that Byron was
ready to assume the responsibilities of leadership; though he
was actually to take them up in a different war and a different
country. There is much splendid verse in praise of liberty
scattered about *Childe Harold* and *Don Juan*, and much denunciation of its destroyers, especially "the intellectual eunuch
Castlereagh", whom Byron and Shelley saw (unjustly) as the
symbol of all that was cold, cruel and oppressive in the post-war
regime.

> Cold-blooded, smooth-faced, placid miscreant!
> Dabbling his sleek young hands in Erin's gore,
> And then for wider carnage taught to pant,
> Transferred to gorge upon a sister shore,
> The vulgarest tool that tyranny could want,
> With just enough of talent and no more,
> To lengthen fetters by another fixed,
> And offer poison long already mixed.[8]

Southey, as the laureate of reaction (and worse, a renegade,
since he had once been a Jacobin), was the object of Byron's
special literary detestation; and the major fruit of this was his
most savagely comic satire, *The Vision of Judgment*. Southey
had written an absurd panegyric of the same name on the death
of George III. Byron's satire envelops both the monarch and
his celebrant in inextinguishable ridicule. The satiric method is
strikingly different from that of the eighteenth century. Pope's
highly finished portraits, by their very finish and the labour
expended on them, confer a certain importance on their subjects. Byron's slapdash manner, by its very carelessness, con-
veys contempt; and a certain tough good humour implies that
his victims are not even worth losing one's temper about. And,

like *Don Juan*, the poem is greatly enriched by the variety of mood. A savage sense of the folly and vanity of the funeral pomps is conveyed in the final couplet of the stanza on George III's funeral:

> It seemed the mockery of hell to fold
> The rottenness of eighty years in gold:

and the stately courtesy of the meeting between St. Peter and Satan is curiously moving, in contrast to the flippant treatment of the celestial personages before it.

In all the astonishing productivity of the Ravenna period, 1820–1, nothing is really central except this poem. With strange pertinacity Byron composed four tragedies, though he had obviously very little instinct for the stage or for the truly dramatic. *Marino Faliero* and *The Two Foscari* are on Venetian themes; *Sardanapalus* is ancient Assyrian; and *Werner* German, of the time of the Thirty Years' War. The two Venetian tragedies are correct but cold compositions: indeed none of the tragedies seems to have any real organic principle—they quicken into temporary life when some facet of Byron's own temperament is touched. *Marino Faliero* revives his sense of being rejected by his own caste, and attempts not very successfully to include private resentment in a passion for public liberty. *Sardanapalus* is more consistently alive in style and more original in conception, though Sardanapalus himself is an impossible figure as a tragic hero. He seems to embody the soft, effeminate and indulgent side of Byron's nature, and to offer an explanation, even an apology for it. In this he achieves a certain touching dignity.

In other places Byron's obsessions are less successfully objectified. *The Deformed Transformed* is a dramatic fragment too obviously, it would seem, inspired by his own lameness, in which the deformed hero becomes a Faustian, daemonic figure. The verse is poor and the conception incomplete. *Cain*, described as a "mystery", is perhaps his most unhappy attempt at dealing with the struggle of good and evil. His defiant resentment of authority found an appropriate object in the political sphere; but he has a very earthly mind, and the attempt to transfer his defiance to the heavens only shows that his ardours, hot and brilliant as they are in the world of men, become ineffectual fires when they reach the *flammantia moenia mundi*. This is not a universal opinion; Scott said, "He has certainly matched Milton on his own ground". But Scott was a better friend than critic. In fact, ultimate impiety is not in Byron's nature. There were qualities and powers before which he felt humble: but what their status in the universe might be he was not able to determine: as long as that uncertainty persists, he must revolt against a world in which his values seem so neglected and insecure: yet as long as those values persist, there must be limits to his cosmic revolt. *Cain* does not attempt to go beyond them: and the drama ends, not in defiance, but in that most unhappy and undramatic of conclusions, a hopeless and ineffectual repentance.

Byron's last journey and his death in the cause of Greek independence cannot be recounted here. That moving combination of nobility, futility and romantic *panache* does not lend itself to summary. But for once Byron was on the winning side; he died, but his cause triumphed, and he remains one of its heroes. For the whole of the nineteenth century he remained a portent and a symbol, whom it was possible to worship or to condemn, but never to neglect. Matthew Arnold, writing in 1852, when Byron's reputation was at its lowest, contrasts two types of humanity; the one who give their lives to some unmeaning taskwork; the other, surely drawn from Byron and intended in part to represent him, who escape their prison and set out again on the ocean of life:

> There the freed prisoner, where'er his heart
> Listeth, will sail;
> Nor does he know how there prevail,
> Despotic on life's sea,
> Trade-winds that cross it from eternity.
>
>   Awhile he holds some false way, undebarred
> By thwarting signs, and braves
> The freshening wind and blackening waves.

And then the tempest strikes him, and between
The lightning bursts is seen
Only a driving wreck,
And the pale master on his spar-strewn deck
With anguished face and flying hair
Grasping the rudder hard,
Still bent to make some port he knows not where
Still standing for some false impossible shore.[9]

NOTES

CHAPTER III. BYRON

1. On the Byronic hero *v*. Mario Praz, *The Romantic Agony*, 1933, 2nd edn. 1951.

2. But *v*. G. Wilson Knight, *Lord Byron's Marriage*, 1957.

3. *Letters and Journals*, IV, 54.

4. ibid. IV, 49.

5. ibid. IV, 59.

6. *Prospectus and Specimen of an Intended National Work*, by William and Robert Whistlecraft; 1817. This was a mock-Arthurian poem by Frere, later expanded into *The Monks and the Giants*.

7. On this question of sources, see E. F. Boyd, *Byron's 'Don Juan': A Critical Study* (1945).

8. *Letters and Journals*, V, 161.

9. ibid. 163.

10. *Don Juan*, Dedication, XII.

11. *A Summer Night.*

CHAPTER IV

SHELLEY

I. SHELLEY AND GODWIN

Too much Shelley criticism has been biography in disguise. The contradictions and controversies of his life are apparently inexhaustible; but his poetry is not so closely bound up with circumstance as Wordsworth's or Byron's. Daily experience shaped and altered their thought; to Shelley it meant little. He is the solitary intellectual. His ideas come from his own mental processes, from study, from visions of the future or dreams of the past, not from the world around him: and he pays the penalty by isolation from the world. A sentimentalized picture of him has often obscured his sheer intellectual attainments. His reading, as his friend Hogg tells us, was enormous.[1]

"No student ever read more assiduously. . . . I never beheld eyes that devoured the pages more voraciously than his. . . . It is no exaggeration to say that out of the twenty-four hours he frequently read sixteen. . . . Few were aware of the extent and fewer still of the profundity of his reading."

His poetry is interwoven with innumerable threads of earlier literature, of philosophy, of science. His prose shows not only a great range of learning, but considerable power of argument and exposition, and his letters reveal for the most part a rather arid doctrinaire intelligence. Yet nearly all the contacts of this vivid and subtle mind with the outer world show a certain failure of adaptation. His reactions, political, social and personal, are violent; but very slightly related to the object that inspired them. The result is a strange gaseous force, overwhelming to some, to others tenuous and unreal.

He was born in 1792, four years after Byron, and in the

same social class. He was the son of a conventional and rather foolish country gentleman and was educated at Eton in the tough days of Keate. A hard upbringing for a sensitive eccentric; and he reacted by alternate withdrawal and revolt. His childhood was filled with games of enchantment, the composition of terrifying romances and magico-scientific experiments—all revealing a mind to whom the realest objects were the denizen of its own unconscious. Haunted by imagery from within and harassed by the outer world, Shelley early felt the need for an intellectual order strong enough to withstand both pressures. He found it in the current revolutionary philosophy. There seems little connection between the venerable eleutherarchs, death-demons and vampires of Shelley's boyish imagination and the world of the mathematical Condorcet or the rationalist Godwin. It is the paradox of the young Shelley that he lives half in a world of anarchic fancy, half in the straitest of philosophical waistcoats. His early reading was mostly in the classics English poetry and a miscellaneous assortment of fantastic and imaginative literature. At Oxford he began to study philosophy and the moral sciences, and was drawn into the international stream of rationalist revolutionary thought. The sources were mainly French: in England the man who had made the most scholastic summing-up of this moral tradition was Godwin. We have already seen him playing a part in Wordsworth's development: Shelley now conceived a fervent devotion to him. Godwin's philosophic anarchism led Shelley and Hogg into a crusade against organized religion and organized society. The result was a pamphlet, *The Necessity of Atheism*, for which they were sent down from Oxford. Emboldened by the feeling that he had suffered in the cause of freedom, Shelley introduced himself to his master in 1812.

"The name of Godwin has been used to excite in me feelings of reverence and admiration. I have been accustomed to consider him a luminary too dazzling for the darkness which surrounds him. From the earliest period of my knowledge of his principles I have ardently desired to share on the footing of intimacy that intellect which I have delighted to contemplate in its emanations. . . . I have just entered on the scene of human operations: yet my feelings and my reasonings correspond with what yours were. My course has been short but eventful. I have seen much of human prejudice, suffered much from human persecution, yet I see no reason hence inferable which should alter my wish for their renovation. . . . Is it strange that, defying prejudice as I have done, I should outstep the limits of custom and prescription, and endeavour to make my desire useful by a friendship with William Godwin?"[2]

The further history of Shelley's association with Godwin is a matter for biography. Its first and most obvious poetical fruit was *Queen Mab*. This seems to have been begun in 1810, when Shelley was eighteen, and it was finished two years later. Until long after his death it remained the most popular of his poems, being especially influential in working-class radical circles. Shelley only printed a few copies for private circulation; Mary Shelley, his first editor, doubted whether he would have included it among his collected works, and certainly he tried to prevent its circulation later in life. Partly on this account, partly because of its obvious crudities, it has had a subordinate place in the Shelley canon, and is commonly written off as versified Godwin, but it is actually a good deal more than this. There is wide and varied reading behind *Queen Mab*, as the notes attest; and much of the inspiration is actually from Holbach. The poem has weak patches, but for the most part it is powerfully written; and it expounds a system which Shelley later enriched, but never abandoned. With its assembly of ideas from Locke, Hume, Rousseau, Holbach and Godwin, it serves also as a convenient poetical handbook to the philosophy of the Enlightenment.

The structure of the poem owes something to Volney's *Ruins*; but it is very naïve, and illustrates Shelley's way of clothing an incompletely human philosophy in fanciful and ethereal form. Ianthe, a lovely young girl, is visited in sleep by the fairy Mab, who takes her on a journey through interstellar space, and reveals to her the history of the past, the actual state

of the world, and the secrets of the future. The cosmos is a
pantheist one, the movements of the stars are the fulfilment of
Eternal Nature's law; and this, not any external deity, is the
ultimate power in the Universe. The view of human history is
largely Godwinian,[3] but with a good deal that derives directly
from Godwin's own sources. Godwin, like many radical
reformers, believed that his generation was just beginning to
clear up the mess of all the preceding centuries. History is therefore a record of crimes and miseries. This was partially relieved
for a brief episode in Athens and Rome; but a still grosser
darkness was to succeed:

> Where Athens, Rome and Sparta stood
> There is a moral desert now.
> Where Cicero and Antoninus lived
> A cowled and hypocritical monk
> Prays, curses and deceives.   (II, 162)

Superstition, embodied in the priest, is one root of evil:
the other is the exercise of power, embodied in the king:

> The King, the wearer of a gilded chain,
> That binds his soul to abjectness, the fool
> Whom courtiers nickname monarch, whilst a slave
> Even to the basest appetites.   (III, 30)

All authority of one being over another is evil.

>   The man
> Of virtuous soul commands not nor obeys.
> Power, like a devastating pestilence
> Pollutes whate'er it touches.   (III, 174)

Yet every heart contains the germ of perfection.

> Every slave, now dragging through the filth
> Of some corrupted city his sad life,
> Pining with famine, swol'n with luxury   (V, 147)

—might imitate the wisest of the sages of the earth. The opera-
tive word is "might". Might—in what circumstances? The
conditional sentence requires a consequent clause, which never

makes a satisfactory appearance. Every heart contains perfection's germ: what, then, prevents its burgeoning? Why is history the dismal record of crime and misery? In Godwin, the answer is delusively clear. The evil lies in "positive institutions" —all the organizations, all the organs of authority that man has created, political and religious. But man, as a pre-Godwinian philosopher remarked, is a political animal; a creature, precisely, of the kind that throws up these institutions. How can this consort with the natural goodness which for Shelley and Godwin is a dogma? The question is never satisfactorily resolved. In Godwin, evil though omnipresent is an accident which education will dispel: men act as they believe, and if but rightly informed, will act rightly too: an opinion also held by the early Socrates, but one startlingly at variance with the general moral experience of mankind.

Shelley's own answer is shifting and uncertain, as though no belief that could be formally expressed really corresponds to his deeper convictions. In one of the notes to *Queen Mab* the origin of moral evil is ascribed to the consumption of animal food; but even to Shelley this must later have seemed an oversimplification. At times he seems to preach the pure Godwinian doctrine; and it is certainly ascribed to him by Mary Shelley. But in fact the natural cast of his imagination seems rather to have been Manichaean; the forces of light, which are fundamental, natural and must in the end prevail, are at the same time opposed by a force of evil, which is just as strongly felt and, as far as the historical imagination can see, eternally recurrent. Its origin and status Shelley never succeeds in defining, or even in symbolizing adequately. It is not nature, it is kings, priests and statesmen who "blast the human flower even in its tenderest bud"; and this "unnatural line of drones" springs from "vice, black loathsome vice"; and the root of vice is venality and covetousness, and they in turn arise from— I know not what. For the most part, Shelley is too concerned with castigating and denouncing evil to inquire into its metaphysical status; and the hall-mark of his poetry is the black-and-white opposition between the world of ideal beauty, freedom and virtue which is to come, and the almost unrelieved

darkness of the past and present state of things. There is no
bridge or explicable connexion between them; we pass in a
sort of momentary trance from one world to the other, a feat
which is not too difficult for the Jacobin poet, but leaves his
exhausted political successors to explain why the arrival of the
New Jerusalem has been unavoidably delayed.

The one possible link between present miseries and the
glorious future is the appearance of a saviour.

> Yes, crime and misery are in yonder earth,
>   Falsehood, mistake and lust;
>   But the eternal world
> Contains at once the evil and the cure.
> Some eminent in virtue shall start up
>   Even in perversest time:
> The truth of their pure lips that never die
> Shall bind the scorpion falsehood with a wreath
>   Of ever-living flame
> Until the monster sting itself to death.   (VI, 29)

Yet the Saviour the world has acknowledged was but a false
prophet.[4] Ahasuerus, the wandering Jew of legend, is summoned
by Mab to tell his story.

> Humbly he came
> Veiling his horrible godhead in the shape of man.
>   He led
> The crowd; he taught them justice, truth and peace
> In semblance, but he lit within their souls
> The quenchless flames of zeal, and blest the sword
> He brought on earth to satiate with the blood
> Of truth and freedom his malignant soul.   (VII, 163)

It is the religion he founded

> Who peoplest earth with demons, hell with men
> And heaven with slaves.

The true sacrificial hero is the atheist whose fate is described by Ianthe herself in a powerful passage. At the end of it Mab replies that there is no God indeed.

Nature confirms the faith his death-groan sealed.

An inexorable natural order called, in the system of Holbach and Godwin, Necessity is the true ruler of the Universe.

> Spirit of Nature! all-sufficing power,
> Necessity! thou mother of the world!
> Unlike the God of human error, thou
> Requir'st no prayers or praises; the caprice
> Of man's weak will belongs no more to thee
> Than do the changeful passions of his breast
> To thy unvarying harmony.   (VI, 196)

There is little in Shelley's later writing that would require him to recant any of this; though there is much to supplement it; and the raw violence in the treatment of the sanctities of others does not reappear. Much of what is to come—the Prometheus myth, tender or heroic according to Shelley's mood, is faintly suggested in the passage about the Saviour quoted above. "The eternal world"—the world of pre-existing Platonic ideas which was to become increasingly real to him, contains both evil and the remedy for evil—the saviour, who by some process that is never explained, will cause the evil to sting itself to death, leaving the good alone, and earth joining harmoniously in the music of the spheres. And the moving power of this regeneration is to be love.

So far we have had the exposition, somewhat cold and mechanical, but powerful and objective, of the radical anarchic creed. The statements of *Queen Mab* are universal historical propositions, true or false, coloured deeply by the black-and-white political antithesis in Shelley's mind, but not coloured at all by his private experience. The young revolutionary thinker preaches with more complete detachment from the young man who suffers than he was ever to achieve again. In *Alastor* (1815) the purely subjective side of his genius, his fondness for allegorizing his own situation, first appears. Its theme is a frequent one

with Shelley—loneliness. The fragment *To the Moon* illustrates
the projection of his own sense of isolation, the habit, endemic
in Romantic verse, but surely used by no one else so constantly
or so naïvely, of attributing his own state of mind to natural
objects.

> Art thou pale for weariness
> Of climbing heaven and gazing on the earth,
> Wandering companionless
> Among the stars that have a different birth,
> And ever changing like a joyless eye
> That finds no object worth its constancy?

Alastor takes up the theme of isolation. The word in Greek
means an avenging demon; it is not, it would appear, the name
of the hero of the poem. Its subtitle is "The Spirit of Solitude",
and this is the Alastor that pursues the young poet-hero—at
least if we are to believe Shelley's preface: "The poet's self-
centred seclusion was avenged by the furies of an irresistible
passion pursuing him to speedy ruin". It must be confessed
that the moral is less evident in the poem itself, where the hero's
loneliness on earth is viewed with complacency, if not approval.
The poem is a dreamlike allegory of the fate of the poet in the
world. The hero's infancy was nurtured by everything that was
bright and lovely, in nature and in human thought. Having
drunk deep at the fountains of divine philosophy, like Shelley
himself,

> when early youth was past, he left
> His cold fireside and alienated home
> To seek strange truth in undiscovered lands. (75)

He travels vaguely through a dream-geography, visiting the
ruins of the past—Athens, Tyre, Jerusalem and Babylon; then
through Arabia and Persia and the wild Carmanian waste; till
at last in the Vale of Cachmire he has a vision.

> He dreamed a veiled maid
> Sate near him, talking in low solemn tones;
> Her voice was like the voice of his own soul. (151)

He embraces her for a moment and then wakes to find the scene vacant. He sets out to travel through the world in search of her, but finding her nowhere, after many confused wanderings, he dies disappointed. We hear little, if anything, of the "self-centred seclusion" of the preface; the theme is rather the hero's vain search for one "whose voice was as the voice of his own soul". Vain because it was the voice of his own soul, incapable of actual embodiment—a notion which the romantic poets never succeed in grasping. For Shelley the search went on throughout his life and its predestinate impossibility accounts for the curiously dual nature of his personal relations: the delicacy and sensitiveness on the one hand, on the other, the strange callousness by which relations were terminated when they proved after all not to be the embodiment of the ideal. The schoolgirl Harriet whom he married on leaving Oxford for a time spoke with the voice of his own soul—indeed it would have been surprising if she had not, for she was subject to a heavy course of indoctrination. Then, for a time, she had to share her rôle and her household with Miss Hitchener; who shortly afterwards turned out to be not the day-star of Shelley's being, but a brown demon, and had to be got rid of at great trouble and expense. By the time *Alastor* was written poor little Harriet had been superseded by the more commanding attractions of Mary Godwin; and Mary was to see the process repeated, though not again with such tragic results, in half a dozen more ideal or sentimental passions. When not affected by any strong emotion Shelley was capable of great discrimination, even of considerable shrewdness: but the objects of his devotion never became independently existing beings, they remained inveterately a part of his subjectivity. *Alastor* presents the hopelessness of such a position.

The scenic descriptions which make up the bulk of the poem are dreamlike—in the quite literal sense that they are composed of fragments of waking experience transposed and condensed in obedience to interior necessities. Fragments of the Alps, the sea, of English pastoral scenes are confused with passages of purely bookish inspiration to make a series of untraceable wanderings with no intelligible course. Byron takes his two pilgrims, the misanthropic and the amorous, on a perfectly describable journey through named and identified places: Keats's Endymion, like the hero of *Alastor*, goes on phantasmagoric travels, but each individual scene is realized with a profusion of sensuous detail: Shelley's scenes are suggested rather than described, and it is their emotional tone rather than their sensuous exterior to which attention is called. His pictures are tranquil or violent, ghastly or tender, and composed of a few recurring elements—the crags, the stars, the torrents, the forests of his interior landscape, rather than the particularity and variety of nature. Few poets use natural images more than Shelley, yet they rarely exist in their own right. They are symbols of states of mind—unlike the minnows and sweet peas of the early Keats, which are just minnows and sweet peas. No more than the Beloved could Nature become for Shelley an independently existing object.

Queen Mab and *Alastor* have hardly any points of contact But the abstract political passions of the one, and the need for love and human sympathy of the other combine in *The Revolt of Islam* (1817) to produce a long revolutionary narrative in which a tender personal love combines with the abstract Godwinian benevolence. It is one of Shelley's most characteristic concepts—personal love overflowing to become the love of humanity: or the love of humanity concentrating and refining itself in personal love. In the original version of the poem, the lovers were also brother and sister, but this was altered for reasons of discretion. The original form of the story is significant, however: it is another example of the curious romantic fascination with incest. In Shelley's case this has certainly nothing to do with Byronic Satanism. The beloved is apt to appear as a sister in Shelley's imagination because a sister is the closest likeness to oneself. The moon in the lyric quoted above is pale for weariness because she is lonely "among the stars that have a different birth"; and Shelley's wish for the heroine of *Epipsychidion* was "would we two had been twins of the same mother".

The ideal relationship depicted in *The Revolt of Islam* is partly that of brother and sister, partly that of lovers, and partly that of comrades in a great enterprise of liberation. For Laon and Cythna are confederates in a radiant and bloodless revolution. Cythna is in the first place an infinitely tender and loving child; then she becomes the confidante of the hero's revolutionary hopes; and later she comes to precede him in experience as a liberator, and give back the inspiration originally received from him. It seems an unintentional allegory of the process by which Shelley, out of some almost accidental affinity, creates a new being filled with his own hopes and ideals; and then expects it to maintain a separate existence, yet still true to the qualities with which he has endowed it. This is more likely to succeed in a poem than in life. But even in the poem the success is incomplete. The vein of narcissistic fantasy that is the main inspiration of *Alastor* is still present here. The *Revolt of Islam*, according to Shelley's preface, is "a story of human passion . . . diversified with moving and romantic adventures" —almost a novel in verse: but the necessary objectivity is hardly attained. Laon is so much Shelley, and Cythna "the voice of his own soul"; and a sameness of imagery (acutely noted by Leigh Hunt) is a consequence of this peregrination round the same inward landscape, unenriched by any real view of the outer world, the necessary source of novelty and variety. The most striking part of the poem is the symbolical Canto I, which shows up the Manichean tendency in Shelley's thought. It tells of the strife between a serpent and an eagle—the serpent, as in Blake and other antinomian moralists representing the power of good, the eagle "Fear, Hatred, Faith and Tyranny". The struggle between them is eternally recurrent. Whenever mankind strives with its oppressors, whenever Justice and Truth wage war with "custom's hydra brood":

> The Snake and Eagle meet—the world's foundations tremble.

Shelley has not yet found a myth adequate to express his conceptions. The fabulous machinery of *Queen Mab* is a mere makeshift framework for straightforward rhetoric. The story of *Alastor* is very slender, and drowned in beautiful but nebulous description; and the poem does not seem to express the concept announced in the preface. *The Revolt of Islam* succeeds in bringing together the outer and the inner sources of his inspiration, but it does so in the form of a long capricious narrative where his weak sense of structure is only too evident. Shelley's way of writing is naturally symbolical: but there is apt to be a thinness and insubstantiality about symbols that spring too directly from the personal imagination. Even Yeats, in his subtle and sympathetic studies of Shelley, finds that his symbolism has an air of "rootless fantasy" because it has never lived in the mind of a people. An increase of power is evident as soon as he makes use of traditional myth.

ii. PROMETHEUS UNBOUND

Shelley left England in 1818; and the colour and richness of Swiss and Italian scenes did much to fertilize his mind, and to provide a fuller and more varied store of symbols for his speculative intuitions. A renewed reading of the Greek tragedians turned his mind towards the ancient myths. From among other projects he settled on the Prometheus story as a subject for a lyrical drama. In Prometheus Shelley found one of the saviour-figures on whom his imagination loved to dwell. Prometheus had stolen fire from heaven and given it to man, and with a little forcing of the original legend could become the revolutionary "Friend of Humanity" and be made to fit the political myth of Shelley's own time. Yet he was not the product of a private imagination. Embodied already in the play of Aeschylus, he had already become a part of European consciousness, and had the kind of quasi-solidity that belongs to the great figures of ancient myth. In Shelley, therefore, he remains very close to the Aeschylean original—the embodiment of moveless fortitude.

But in Aeschylus there is a problem: the sympathy aroused for the bravery and suffering of Prometheus inevitably presents Zeus as a tyrannical oppressor: and this conflicts with the almost monotheistic exaltation of Zeus as the author of justice that we find elsewhere in Aeschylean tragedy. The *Prometheus Bound* is the first play of a trilogy, and from what we know of the rest it appears that both of these stern and moveless figures in the end modified their position and reached an ultimate reconciliation. This did not suit Shelley's philosophy. "In truth," he says, "I was averse from a catastrophe so feeble as that of reconciling the champion with the oppressor of mankind."[5] Yet though he felt the presence of evil so powerfully it was an essential of the Godwinian system and at least a part of Shelley's formal creed "that evil is not inherent in the system of creation, but an accident that might be expelled."[6] Zeus must be consistently a tyrant, but he must disappear, and Prometheus must be unequivocally victorious. The substance of the Aeschylean drama is contained in Shelley's first act. The rest of the play is concerned with the overthrow of Jupiter and the liberation of Prometheus. And other characters and other motives appear, only faintly foreshadowed in Aeschylus.

Prometheus is the spouse of Asia and she, with her sisters Panthea and Ione, daughters of Ocean, are, as in Aeschylus, spirits of sympathy and tenderness. Asia in a special sense represents the spirit of love. It is probably a mistake to fit the poem out with a set of symbolical equations, but we can perhaps say that Prometheus, besides being the Titan of legend, symbolizes the aspiring and enduring spirit of humanity, and that Asia represents love, with which, when the liberation is complete, humanity will be reunited. In the first act she is exiled from Prometheus, waiting in a lonely valley. Prometheus, chained to his rock, suffering but defiant, begs Earth his mother for a repetition of the words with which he has defied Jupiter. In order that his own lips and the lips of those who love him shall not be defiled by a curse, the phantasm of Jupiter is called up from the shades to repeat the words of Prometheus' execration (I, 262). By this curious device the hatred and defiance that is necessary to the good characters, yet in some sense inconsistent with their goodness, is itself fathered on the oppressor. Prometheus repents the bitterness of his imprecation.

It doth repent me, words are quick and vain;
Grief for a while is blind, and so was mine.
I wish no living thing to suffer pain.   (I, 303)

Mercury and the Furies appear in their traditional rôle of
intensifying Prometheus' sufferings; and a chorus of spirits
conclude the act by prophesying obscurely the ultimate
triumph of love.

In the second act Asia takes the leading part, and becomes
the prophet and the instrument of the liberation. She dreams
that their lot is about to change; and she and Panthea are
summoned by spirit voices to an unknown journey. The
scenery is again visionary with shifting prismatic colours and
evanescent glimpses of pastoral or mountain landscapes.
Though they melt dreamlike into one another, the individual
pictures are more clearly realized than in *Alastor*. The attendant
fauns and spirits who surround the active characters inhabit a
world of natural fantasy; they belong to no accepted mythology;
yet they are a vital part of the poem. Surrounding the characters
whose life and being are moral, they represent the world of
wayward impersonal forces, the bright inhuman spirits of
nature, which are also part of Shelley's vision, and furnish
much of its strange loveliness.

I have heard those more skilled in spirits say,
The bubbles, which the enchantment of the sun
Sucks from the pale faint water-flowers that pave
The oozy bottom of clear lakes and pools,
Are the pavilions where such dwell and float
Under the green and golden atmosphere
Which noontide kindles through the woven leaves;
And when these burst, and the thin fiery air,
The which they breathed within those lucent domes,
Ascends to flow like meteors through the night,
They ride on them, and rein their headlong speed,
And bow their burning crests, and glide in fire
Under the waters of the earth again.   (II, ii, 70)

This seems to be a quasi-scientific account of the origin of the *ignis fatuus,* or will o' the wisp: and Shelley is perhaps the first to domesticate such concepts in poetry. The struggle and the victory of Prometheus are not everything, and his liberation is not the only source of happiness; much of the spontaneous joy is in these passages of natural magic, in which nature is not seen as something opposed to moral activity, but as the lovely matrix from which moral activity arises.

The journey of Asia and Panthea takes them to the cave of Demogorgon—a mysterious being, only seen as "a mighty darkness, filling the seat of power". Jupiter is the present ruler of the world, but in Demogorgon we see an echo of the idea, immanent in Greek tragedy, of Moira or Fate, as stronger than the gods. Demogorgon is a power who stands behind the other beings in the play: we have met him before in *Queen Mab* under the colder title of Necessity. In a dialogue with Asia he ascribes the creation of the living world (Nature), as well as thought, passion, reason, will (moral experience) to "merciful God". But when asked who made terror, madness, crime, remorse, he will only reply obscurely "He reigns". The whole dialogue is designedly oracular, and to paraphrase this central passage of the poem is inevitably to deform it; but an answer to Asia's questions dimly shapes itself. Jupiter is the supreme of living things, but he is only a demiurge, his hour will come. Indeed, no sooner is Asia made aware of this than the hour *is* come. The Spirit of the Hour appears. Asia and Panthea mount his chariot, and pass on another strange journey through clouds and over the tops of mountains. Asia becomes transfigured before the eyes of her sister, and spirits address her in an entranced hymn.

> Life of Life! thy lips enkindle
>   With their love the breath between them;
> And thy smiles before they dwindle
>   Make the cold air fire; then screen them
> In those looks, where whoso gazes
>   Faints, entangled, in their mazes.

Child of light! thy limbs are burning
   Through the vest which seems to hide them;
As the radiant lines of morning
   Through the clouds ere they divide them;
And this atmosphere divinest
   Shrouds thee wheresoe'er thou shinest.
(II, v, 48)

Jupiter's hour is also her hour. The destruction of tyranny
is accompanied by an expansion of the realm of love.

The first brief scene of Act III sees the actual downfall of
Jupiter. He proclaims his omnipotence: but no sooner are the
words out than the car of the hour arrives: Demogorgon
descends and advances towards him, and Jupiter simply falls.
The conflict is not externalized or elaborated: from being an
all-powerful ruler, Jupiter just disappears: his hour is come,
and that is all. Just so in Shelley's political philosophy there is
no bridge between the actual state of misery and oppression
and the new glad world that is to come. When the time is ripe
the one will be transformed on to the other: the gap in the
dramatic action of Prometheus corresponds to an actual gap in
Shelley's thinking.

The downfall accomplished, Heracles frees Prometheus,
Prometheus is reunited with Asia, Earth is rejuvenated, disease
and pain disappear, and death becomes a mother's evening
embrace. The world of mutability is purged and rejuvenated
by the loving acceptance of its conditions; toads and snakes
and efts become beautiful, yet with little change of shape or
hue, and the kingfisher feeds unharmed on nightshade berries.
The spirit of the Hour re-enters and describes what he has seen
in the world of men.

      . . . but soon I looked
And behold, thrones were kingless, and men walked
One with another, even as spirits do;
None fawned, none trampled. . . .
The loathsome mask has fallen, the man remains,
Sceptreless, free, uncircumscribed, but man—
(III, iv, 130)

The fourth act was an afterthought,[7] a lyrical rhapsody in which the powers of Nature, the Earth and the Moon, hours and spirits rejoice at their liberation. It is not, however, unrelated to Shelley's deepest thought. The moral regeneration of the world through love is in his system also accompanied by a physical regeneration; nature takes part equally in the redemption. Shelley was not indeed inclined to separate natural and spiritual forces. Professor Grabo has shown[8] that Shelley echoes or seems to echo Newton's identification of electrical energy with a quasi-immaterial "Spirit of the Universe", which is also the physical expression of that which in the moral sphere is love. It is hard to accept all these speculations and harder still for literary students to accept Whitehead's judgement of Shelley's scientific preoccupations.

"What the hills were to the youth of Wordsworth, a chemical laboratory was to Shelley. It is unfortunate that Shelley's literary critics have, in this respect, so little of Shelley in their own mentality. They tend to treat as a casual oddity of Shelley's nature what was, in fact, part of the main structure of his mind, permeating his poetry through and through. If Shelley had been born a hundred years later, the twentieth century would have seen a Newton among chemists."[9]

To the shoemaker there is nothing like leather: but the literary critic, to give that unscientific observer his due, is perhaps more likely than the scientist in a literary moment to notice how fragmentary and capricious were Shelley's dealings with science. The important substratum of truth in this way of thinking about Shelley is that he does not see a dualism between material and spiritual life; each is one aspect of the same reality; and the rejuvenation of the one can only be accomplished (though not by any process expressible in scientific terms) by the parallel regeneration of the other. Thus the cosmic and natural imagery of *Prometheus* is not inessential to it, an additional lyrical rhapsodizing, as is sometimes said: it is a vital part of the whole imaginative concept.

Of course a poem conceived in this way is not likely to obey the rules of ordinary dramatic construction. (Neither does the *Promethus* of Aeschylus for that matter.) Aristotelian peripeteias and recognitions are human, all too human devices for poetry conceived on a cosmic scale. *Prometheus Unbound* is the first of a long line of nineteenth-century poems cast in dramatic form, but with no conceivable relation to the theatre. Indeed drama in the ordinary sense was not the direction in which Shelley's work tended. The realization of his own conceptions was too personal and too intense to allow the "negative capability", the ability to become everything and everyone, that the dramatist requires; and his constructive weakness is far more damaging here than in other forms. His one attempt at a stage drama was *The Cenci*. It is surprisingly powerful in character and atmosphere, and direct and concentrated in style: it is also surprisingly unShelleyan. The story, a horrible one of incest and revenge, seems very little related to the main lines of Shelley's thought; the dramatic structure is extremely weak and disordered; and most of its striking passages are derivative, largely from Shakespeare and Webster, as Shelley never is elsewhere. It appears from the preface that he is extremely conscious of attempting what is for him an unusual kind of composition:

> "I have endeavoured as nearly as possible to represent the characters as they probably were, and have sought to avoid the error of making them actuated by my own conceptions of right and wrong, false or true. .... I have avoided with great care in writing this play the introduction of what is commonly called mere poetry. ...."

Heroic self-denial, indeed, but the result is to produce only a diversion from the main line of Shelley's work. A later dramatic poem, *Hellas*, is described by Shelley as "a mere improvise"; and though much slighter it is really more congenial to him. It celebrates the opening of the Greek revolt, in a form suggested by the *Persae* of Aeschylus. Shelley's sympathy with a contemporary struggle for freedom unites with his adoration of ancient Greece; and the two are fused into a visionary hope for the restoration of Hellenic glories in the famous final chorus.

iii.　SHELLEY AS A LYRIST.

To many readers Shelley's genius is primarily lyrical: which commonly implies emotional. This is very doubtful—intense and unremitting intellectual activity seems to have been the main characteristic of his mind. The slender wisps of song that are perhaps the most familiar of Shelley's works were mostly written in moments of dejection or emotional abandonment. About half a dozen of them are exquisite; but many pages of Shelley's work are occupied with such brief lyrical fragments; and outside the famous anthology pieces most of them are bad. Many readers of *O World, O Life, O Time* and *Music, When Soft Voices Die* imagine that there is a great deal more on the same level. In fact there is very little. More characteristic of Shelley is the longish, elaborated poem, lyrical in spirit, though not in form. This may be outwardly elegy, like *Adonais*; narrative, like *The Sensitive Plant*; a love-rhapsody, like *Epipsychidion*; or a fragment of a fairy tale, like *The Witch of Atlas*: but all exhibit the same mixture of speculation, the elaboration of a private mythology, and the element of song. Midway between the two in scale and complexity are *The Cloud, To a Skylark*, the *Lines Written in the Euganean Hills* and the *Ode to the West Wind*. Two formal odes, very much in the eighteenth-century manner, *Naples* and *Liberty*, make a rather disconcerting appearance: very competent performances of their kind, but hard to fit in to the prevailing picture of Shelley's genius.

Shelley's command of melopoeia, musical suggestion, the use of words as song, is at its best exquisite; but it is capricious. Or rather, command is not the word. "Poetry," he says in the *Defence*, "differs in this respect from logic, that it is not subject to the active powers of the mind, and that its birth and recurrence have no necessary connexion with the consciousness or will." His most delicate music comes unsuspected like a wandering breeze, usually associated with some intense feeling, abstracted from particular circumstance. The hymn to Asia,

"Life of Life," in *Prometheus*, is one example; the last chorus
of *Hellas* is another. Both are ecstatic; the first a vision quiver-
ing with brilliant light, the second a serener glow. Sometimes
it is despondency that awakens Shelley's Aeolian harp.

> Out of the day and night
> A joy has taken flight.
> Fresh spring, and summer and winter hoar
> Move my faint heart with grief, but with delight
> No more, O never more.[10]

On the level of easier emotion, this uncertain instrument
breathes a melodious sentimentality that sometimes recalls
Tom Moore.

> Though the sound overpowers,
> Sing again, with your dear voice revealing
> A tone
> Of some world far from ours,
> Where music and moonlight and feeling
> Are one.[11]

It is worth mentioning this, for Shelley is so often seen as
"pinnacled dim in the intense inane" that too much has been
claimed for poems that themselves make no such claims: and
this in turn has called forth quite unnecessary blasts of deprecia-
tion. Many of his shorter lyrics are occasional poems, like *The
Aziola*, which is charming; or *With a guitar, to Jane*, which is
less so. At times—we can see it in this poem, in the *Lines Written
in the Euganean Hills*—a kind of rhythmical automatism seems
to overtake him:

> For it had learned all harmonies
> Of the plains and of the skies
> Of the forest and the mountains
> And the many-voiced fountains
> The clearest echoes of the hills
> The softest note of falling rills
> The melodies of birds and bees
> The murmuring of summer seas.[12]

There seems no reason why the catalogue should ever end, and he seems to be going on largely because he does not know how to stop. Octosyllabics are particularly liable to bring on these attacks; but it may happen with any of the more facile measures —there is a good deal of it in *Epipsychidion*. Which means not only that Shelley's musical gift is a shy and uncertain visitant, but that he has no certain command of style when it is absent.

The same contrast is found if we look at his images and structure. *Ozymandias* is an extremely clear and direct poem, advancing to a predetermined end by means of one firmly held image. "When the lamp is shattered", a poem that has been both admired and condemned, proceeds in a wholly different way. Images are put together, often in no logically comprehensible sequence. The series of analogies—light will not survive the shattering of the lamp, music the breaking of the instrument—are all piled up to illustrate the statement that

> The heart's echoes render
> No song when the spirit is mute.

But there is nothing within the context of the poem (and I have not been able to discover anything outside it) to tell us what this means. Many of the succeeding images are kept together only by a community of emotional tone. Yet the poem does make a unified impression, in spite of the extremely loose relation of its parts. A demand for "metaphysical" clarity would be quite out of place here. Poems can attain unity by more than one means; and among the possibilities is that of retaining vaguely connected images in an informal pattern, floating, as it were, on a breeze of rhythm and music. This air-borne dance has always been recognized as one of Shelley's especial achievements. (The last act of *Prometheus* is a supreme example.) But the breeze has only to flag, and the whole becomes a heap of jarring atoms, or the spasmodic scurrying of loose papers in an idle gust.

The *Skylark* has great beauty in individual stanzas; it has been pointed out that the order of the stanzas is insignificant

—they could be rearranged almost anyhow without loss. This is not as damaging as is sometimes supposed: it is in fact a not unusual poetic situation: it is not obligatory for poems to progress in a temporal or logical sequence; they have often a timeless, synoptic point of view; and this is appropriate enough to a poem about the song of a far-off, almost unseen bird. But the *Skylark* is rather a long lyric: and the absence of internal structure is more felt the longer a poem becomes. And it remains true that a more conscious designer than Shelley would either have given the poem a clearer sense of direction, or have made it a shorter poem.

The process in much of Shelley's lyric poetry is to find in natural objects a symbol for his own emotional patterns. His best poetry arises when one of his major passions finds an adequate symbol; as it does in the *Ode to the West Wind*. The wind does not become, like the moon in the fragment quoted earlier, an arbitrary projection of an emotional state. It exists in its own right, as a destroyer and preserver, sweeping away the old in storms, and gently fostering the new with zephyrs. Thus it becomes linked with another symbolism—the cycle of the seasons. The poem begins with autumn and ends with spring, or the foretaste of spring: and the wind is the spirit of destruction and regeneration, the common power that moves through both. The theme of death and rebirth, destruction and regeneration, is doubly powerful to Shelley: first it is the great natural process of which political revolution is the human and social example; and secondly because it affords an escape from the crushing personal despondency with which he was so often afflicted, which bring about his not infrequent lapses into mere self-pity.

The death and rebirth themes are announced in the opening stanza. The wind drives away the dead leaves and conducts the seeds, apparently cold and dead, to their graves; but the graves are also cradles in which they are to be reborn in the spring. The second stanza pictures the wind in its stormy and terrible aspect. The third opens with an iridescent picture of the other west wind, the Zephyrus or Favonius of the ancients, who produced flowers and fruit by the sweetness of his breath. It is a shimmering, Turneresque Mediterranean scene. But the stanza concludes with a return of the spirit of terror—the same wind which ruffles the surface of the Mediterranean also cleaves the Atlantic into chasms and frightens the submerged vegetation of the ocean. These three stanzas are built up on the antithesis between the two powers of the wind—its terrifying powers of destruction and its gentle fostering influence. They are descriptive, the imagery is largely visual, and the arrangement is a symmetrical one of contrasts of light and shade. The dark tones and brilliant sombre colours of the opening lines are contrasted with the lightness and softness of the lines on spring in the latter half of the stanza. Stanza two is all dark with brilliant flashes: and stanza three reverses the order of stanza one—the soft, light-toned Mediterranean picture giving place to the sombre depths of the Atlantic.

These three stanzas are something like the octave of a sonnet, announcing and elaborating a theme. The fourth and fifth stanzas are like the sestet, reflective and personal applications of the theme. The impression of the first three stanzas has been one of unimpeded energy and power: and it has been quite objective and impersonal. The poet and his sensibility have made no individual appearance. In the fourth stanza his own sense of oppression and constraint is related to the wind's freedom and strength. He would like to be a dead leaf, a cloud or a wave to be swept along by the wind's power; yet once he had been able to imagine that the wind's power was his own: and a similar power is naturally and by right his own: he too is tameless and swift, but has been crushed by the weight of the world.

At this point we might be on the way to more stanzas written in dejection. The wind is a power of destruction; and in his despondency the poet could wish to be swept away by it like a dead leaf. But that is not the final direction the poem is to take: the wind is also a power of regeneration, and so it can be to him. The last stanza is a prayer that it may be so. Why pray to an insentient natural force? Mere poetic "personification", to use a crass phrase for what can often be a crass device? No. As a force of death and rebirth the wind is one manifestation

of the creative principle that runs through the whole universe.
Therefore the poet can say

> Make me thy lyre, even as the forest is
> What if my leaves are falling like its own?

—can rightly ask to be used by the creative power even if his
personal life is dejected and decayed. He then takes up the dead
leaf image of the opening lines and gives it a new turn. Destruction, the sweeping away of the old, is necessary before re-
creation can begin; and that is implied in the opening stanza,
for the wind sweeps away leaves and seeds together. But in the
fifth stanza the withered leaves themselves "quicken a new
birth"—they provide the soil in which the new seeds can grow.
Dead thoughts, words which seem useless and unheeded, can
nevertheless nurture a new life. If possessed by the wind, the
creative power, the dead thoughts need not even be dead; and
they become in the next line ashes and sparks, to kindle, not
merely to feed a new conflagration. Death is only the prelude
to renewed life; and the poem ends as it began, with the cycle
of the seasons—

> If Winter comes, can Spring be far behind?

The structure of this ode is quite different from that of a
typical seventeenth-century lyric, which may, as we have been
told, have a logical argument almost syllogistic in completeness.
Nor is there any very close linkage between the individual
images; nor is there any very marked use of the sound effects,
assonances and alliterations, by which some poets organize
their verse. The logic here is the logic of feeling, which has its
own order, and its own possibilities of formal perfection. I have
tried to analyse this structure; but after a poem has been split
up that it may be better understood, it must be put together
again. And the reader's final impression is not of separable
parts, feelings or images, but of a continuous powerful movement, sweeping through the whole. It is in this sense of continuous and directed energy that the *West Wind* is superior to

The Cloud, *The Skylark*, or any other of Shelley's lyrics on the same scale.

Here the principle of organization is entirely his own, without particular literary precedent. *Adonais*, on the death of Keats (1821), is a formal elegy, taking its place in a long tradition of such poems. It includes many features from the Sicilian pastoral elegies of Theocritus, Bion and Moschus, long familiar in the vernacular literatures through poems written in imitation of them. Like *Lycidas*, also in the same tradition, it is inspired by no very vivid sense of personal loss, but takes over a traditional pattern and uses it to express the writer's own preoccupations and his own philosophy. Shelley takes from the Sicilian elegies the machinery of the lament and the summoning of the powers of Nature to mourn for the dead shepherd, as Milton did in *Lycidas*: and as Milton expanded the convention by introducing the awful figure of St. Peter, so Shelley adds to it by introducing the mourning of Urania and the brother poets. Among these he brings in himself:

> one frail form,
> A phantom among men, companionless—

in lines where self-pity seems a little obtrusive. But they again serve to do what Milton did in *Lycidas*, to relate the formal elegy to his own situation and to that of his subject. Adonais has been killed by the world's hostility, and the fellow-poet who celebrates him is exiled by its neglect. Shelley is depicting the fate of the romantic poet in the world of Eldon, Castlereagh and the *Quarterly Review*, as Milton that of the young Puritan poet in the world of Laud and Strafford.

An already consecrated feature of the traditional elegy is the turn at the close: after the lament, the recantation—he is not dead: but the cast which is given to this defiant assertion of immortality depends on the philosophy of the writer, pagan, Christian or modern pantheist. Milton, incurably classic as well as Christian, gives us two versions of the fate of Lycidas—he has become a nature-spirit, the genius of the shore; and he is received among the solemn troops and sweet societies of the

saints in heaven. The Shelleyan immortality foretold for
Adonais is hardly of a personal kind.

> He is made one with Nature: there is heard
> His voice in all her music, from the moan
> Of thunder, to the song of night's sweet bird;
> He is a presence to be felt and known
> In darkness and in light from herb and stone,
> Spreading itself where'er that Power may move
> Which has withdrawn his being to its own;
> Which wields the world with never wearied love,
> Sustains it from beneath, and kindles it above. (XLII)

A sort of pantheism: but Adonais is not, like Wordsworth's
Lucy, simply "rolled round in earth's diurnal course, with
rocks and stones and trees". He has become part of the spirit
which governs the Universe, which *is* the Universe—for Shelley
ends with a Platonic or neo-Platonic or Brahmanistic assertion
that eternity alone is real, that the phenomenal world is an
illusion, is Maya, a veil that hides us from the one true light.

> The One remains, the many change and pass;
> Heaven's light forever shines, Earth's shadows fly;
> Life, like a dome of many-coloured glass
> Stains the white radiance of eternity. (LII)

But it would be a mistake to suppose that Shelley lives
consistently on that plane. Though the world is illusion, it has
a kind of fairy-tale reality in whose dominion his poetry is often
willing to linger: indeed, in which poetry must linger. The
white radiance of eternity leaves the poet with few subjects,

> Struck dumb in the simplicity of fire,

as Yeats puts it. In *The Witch of Atlas* and *The Sensitive Plant*
Shelley is mythologizing, gracefully and half playfully: and the

lines "To Mary" which introduce *The Witch* show that he was willing enough to allow his muse to play.

> What hand would crush the silken-winged fly
> The youngest of inconstant April's minions,
> Because it cannot climb the purest sky,
> Where the swan sings, amid the sun's dominions?

In a study as short as this these diaphanous pieces may be spared the burden of an exposition. *Epipsychidion* (1821), however, claims rather more. It is the fruit of a short-lived passion for a young Italian girl, Emilia Viviani; one of those sudden devotions with which Shelley's life is punctuated; and it is a poem of idealized and ecstatic love. In a fictitious introduction Shelley presents it as the work of a dead friend, and compares it, in its refined and esoteric sentiment, to the *Vita Nuova*. It is prefaced by a seductive Platonic-romantic motto, taken from an essay by Emilia herself:

> "L'anima amante si slancia fuori del creato, e si crea nell' infinito un mondo tutto per essa, diverso assai di questo oscuro e pauroso baratro."

(The soul of the lover flings itself out from the created world, and creates in infinity a world all for itself, far different from this abyss of fear and darkness.)

And this should give us the key to the realm in which the poem moves. Emilia is a "Seraph of Heaven, too gentle to be human"; she is" the veiled Glory of the lampless Universe"; she is a sister, a vestal sister, rather than a mistress: so that when we are told, at the hundredth line, that a ship is waiting in the harbour to bear them away to the Ionian islands we may be fairly sure that what follows is more a piece of fanciful self-indulgence than anything else. Yet the poem contains a good deal of disguised and often obscure autobiography. Mary Shelley appears as the moon, to which Emilia is the sun, and they are to share the poet's life between them. The facility with which Shelley effects the transition from the actual to the ideal plane is disconcerting; the proposition "I do not at present intend to make you my mistress" does not really entail the consequence "This is therefore a great spiritual love." It is probable that opinions will always differ about the value of this kind of sublimation; but I think we can say that it should be both a more arduous and a less conscious process than Shelley seems to contemplate. The verse, too, has the kind of facility that is apt to overtake Shelley when he is possessed by a single one-way passion: and for all its reputation *Epipsychidion* has little importance except as a document of the romantic sensibility.

The last and most obscure fragment of Shelley's verse is the *Triumph of Life* (1822), the poem on which he was engaged at the time of his death. Over five hundred lines exist; but we cannot deduce from them what the ultimate purpose of the poem was to be. The first half of it describes the procession of Life, led by a blind charioteer—a rout of captives in which all humanity is enslaved. In the second half a distorted form which is all that is left of Rousseau explains how, having once seen a brighter vision, he too became enslaved to life. There is much obscurity which the completion of the poem might or might not have removed; and it is not clear whether the sombre view of human destiny so far presented would have been the ultimate one. What is clear is the decision and rapidity of the verse. The poem is written in *terza rima*, and this has suggested the influence of Dante to some commentators. Both Dowden, however, and Shelley's latest biographer, Professor Newman Ivey White, remark what should be obvious, that the actual model is Petrarch's *Trionfi*,[13] especially the Triumph of Love. The spare directness of the style and the clear visualization, quite divorced from the conventionally poetic, is, however, almost Dantesque in places, and is certainly new to Shelley. Even in detail there is much that is obscure, but enough remains to suggest that Shelley at the end of his life may have been on the threshold of a new technical development.

Development, however, is not a word that we naturally use of Shelley's poetry. The characteristic qualities of his mind were fixed early: though his ideas expanded, the fundamentals changed little, and he is not an industrious experimenter in various techniques. He writes as he must, and if he had lived longer it is not likely that the impelling necessities of his poetry would have become very different.

iv. THE DEFENCE OF POETRY

It remains to say something of Shelley's beliefs about the nature and functions of poetry. There is something to be found in the letters (though his letters are not nearly so illuminating as those of Keats); much in the prefatory notes to the poems; but the principal place is the *Defence of Poetry*. There seems always to have been some uncertainty in Shelley's mind between didactic and purely artistic aims; but there is little doubt that the first predominate. The preface to the *Revolt of Islam* describes the poem as an experiment on the public mind to discover "how far a thirst for a happier condition of moral or political society" has survived the tempests of the times. Shelley goes on to say, "I have sought to enlist the harmony of metrical language, the ethereal combinations of the fancy, the rapid and subtle transitions of human passion, all those elements which essentially compose a poem, in the cause of a liberal and comprehensive morality". It will be noted that "all the elements which essentially compose a poem" are enlisted as subordinates in a moral cause that is separate from themselves. Writing to Peacock in January 1819, at the time of the composition of *Prometheus*, Shelley says quite bluntly, "I consider poetry very subordinate to moral and political science". In similar vein he confesses in the preface to *Prometheus* to "a passion for reforming the world": yet adds "it is a mistake to suppose that I dedicate my compositions solely to the direct enforcement of reform. . . . Didactic poetry is my abhorrence; nothing can be equally well expressed in prose that is not tedious and supererogatory in verse". A contradiction is apparent, but it is reconciled in the passage that follows.

"My purpose has hitherto been simply to familiarize the highly refined imagination of the more select classes of poetical readers with beautiful idealisms of moral excellence, aware that until the mind can love and admire and trust, and hope and endure, reasoned principles of moral conduct are seeds cast upon the highway of life which the unconscious passengers trample into dust, although they would bear the harvest of his happiness."

Poetry is to work by its own imaginative processes, but the aim is still to awaken and stimulate the moral sense. From this point of view Shelley never departed, and the *Defence of Poetry* is largely an expansion of it.

The *Defence of Poetry* appeared in 1821. It was originally intended to be a reply to a pamphlet by Peacock, *The Four Ages of Poetry*. This is a brilliant piece of work, satirical and only half serious, which maintains that in the current era of science and philosophy the poet is a relic of primitive barbarism "wallowing in the rubbish of departed ignorance, and raking up the ashes of dead savages to find gewgaws and rattles for the grown babies of the age". Shelley was indignant and resolved to break a lance with him. But what results is something different from a mere answer to Peacock; it is an exalted defence of the honours of poetry and the imagination, an extension of the tradition of Sidney and the Renaissance champions of the Muses, and the best statement in English of the early Romantic theory of poetry. Coleridge attempts to give his ideas a philosophical foundation which Shelley is content to assume; and he is more attractive to the speculative mind because it is never quite clear exactly what he is saying. Wordsworth's preface seems a more massive piece of polemic. But Shelley is a clearer expositor than either of these more celebrated theorists—and he remains a poet even in his prose. The *Defence* is itself a work of art—a claim which could not be made for the prose writings of Wordsworth or Coleridge.

He begins by stating as an axiom what Coleridge tries to prove—the power of the imagination to perceive, in some sense, essential reality with a directness impossible to the discursive faculties. His language here is partly Coleridgean; and since he had read *Biographia Literaria* in the year of its appearance, we need not doubt that this is the source of his theory of the imagination and its functions. Poetry is the expression of the imagination, and it has access, therefore, to this special kind of imaginative knowledge. All men have some imagination, so all are in some degree poets. But there is an absolute standard of beauty, to which every artistic representation approximates more or less closely. The poet is simply the man whose faculties for approximation to this standard are exceptionally great. Since he is able then to express essential truth in the form of beauty, from which all men of uncorrupted taste receive pleasure, the poet is not only the inventor of the arts, but the institutor of laws and the founder of civil society. Without him the beauty of order and the beauty of holiness would never have been perceived; and if their beauty had never been perceived, they would never have been desired. The poet is even a prophet, for by seeing the present as it really is he sees in it the seeds of the future.

A critical passage on the distinction between prose and poetry follows (Shelley does not equate poetry with verse; for him Plato and Bacon are poets); and there is a passage, Aristotelian in origin, but echoed by all the great Romantics, about the universality of poetry. Then succeeds a long panoramic survey of poetry from Homer onwards, which occupies the bulk of the essay. Historical surveys of this kind are apt to date. Shelley's is remarkably fresh; and the whole passage is a testimony to the extent and sensitiveness of his reading. Its purpose is to show the effect of poetry on society, and to show that "the presence or absence of poetry in its most perfect and universal form, has been found to be connected with good or evil in conduct or habit". The reason for this is at the core of Shelley's belief.

"The great secret of morals is love; or a going out of our own nature, and an identification of ourselves with the beautiful which exists in thought, action or person, not our own. A man, to be greatly good, must imagine intensely and comprehensively; he must put himself in the place of another, and of many others; the pains and pleasures of his species must become his own. The great instrument of moral good is the imagination; and poetry ministers to the effect by acting upon the cause."

An objection to many such lofty transcendental claims for poetry is that they fail to account for minor poetry and the lesser kinds. To this Shelley provides an admirable answer. Without interrupting the majestic sweep of his own theory, he does beautiful justice to the more modest kinds of imaginative writing. Such compositions, he says, may be read simply as fragments or isolated portions; but the more perceptive will "recognize them as episodes to that great poem, which all poets, like the co-operating thoughts of one great mind, have built up since the beginning of the world".

In modern times (and here the specific answer to Peacock begins) "poets have been challenged to resign the civic crown to reasoners and mechanists"—on the plea of utility. Shelley opposes this, on hedonist and utilitarian grounds. Utility is whatever conduces to pleasure. But it has a narrow and a wider sense. The first is all that satisfies the mere animal needs, that conduces to transitory pleasure: the second is whatever strengthens and purifies the affections, enlarges the understanding, and conduces to durable and universal pleasure. It is to this second kind of utility that poetry contributes. We owe a debt of gratitude to the philosophers, to Locke, Hume, Gibbon, Voltaire and Rousseau: but if they had never lived

"a little more nonsense would have been talked for a century or two; and perhaps a few more men, women and children burnt as heretics. We might not at this moment be congratulating ourselves on the abolition of the inquisition in Spain;"

—but without the poets and creative artists the moral condition of mankind would be inconceivably degraded; for the analytical reason can itself do nothing to arouse men's generous faculties. The passage which follows has even more relevance today than when it was written.

"We have more moral, political and historical wisdom than we know how to reduce into practice: we have more scientific and economical knowledge than can be accommodated to the just distribution of the produce which it multiplies. . . . There is no want of knowledge respecting what is wisest and best in morals, government and political economy, or at least what is wiser and better than what men now practise and endure. But we want the creative faculty to imagine that which we know; we want the generous impulse to act on that which we imagine; we want the poetry of life. . . .

"The cultivation of poetry is never more to be desired than at periods when, from an excess of the calculating principle, the accumulation of the materials of external life exceed the quantity of the power of assimilating them to the internal laws of human nature."

It is evident enough that by this time poetry has become something very different from making verses. It includes all the means by which the sympathetic and generous emotions are aroused. But of these the arts are the chief. Since imagination shows us the real nature of the world it inevitably takes us out of the small circle of self-regarding feeling. Since it sounds the depths of human nature it shows not only the goings on in the poet's mind, but in the mind of the age, and can see in them the germs of the future. Hence when Shelley in his final paragraph calls the poets "the mirrors of the gigantic shadows which futurity casts upon the present", he is not merely using a rhetorical phrase, but expressing a real conviction—that the poet's intuitions often show him the direction in which the world is moving more clearly than the speculations of the political philosopher. And it would not be hard to find examples to substantiate this claim. But from this we pass to the final phrase: "Poets are the unacknowledged legislators of the world"; we look forward into the succeeding century and observe that if the poets are legislators they have some very formidable competitors—soldiers, historians, economists, physicists. All that Shelley says about the gap between our natural science and our moral ability to use it is manifestly true—but is it really the business of poetry to bridge the gulf?

Many later nineteenth-century writers agreed that it was. Poetry, for Arnold, is to replace religion as the guide and teacher of mankind: for Pater and his successors, art itself is to become a sort of religion. Shelley's argument is more reasoned and his position stronger than theirs. It is a poor thing not to feel the purity and generosity of his enthusiasm; but there is, after all, a fallacy in the Romantic apology for poetry, as in all later attempts to save the world by literature; two senses of the word poetry are confused. Poetry as the whole imaginative and sympathetic life of man is one thing; poetry the work of art is another; and to transfer what is true of the first bodily to the second is only rhetorically effective. In Shelley's philosophical system there is always a gap between the wretched actuality and the radiant and possible ideal. In some of his expository prose writing, he is prepared to fill it laboriously by the methods of patient reformism. But his imagination was more impatient: the gap must be bridged by a spark, and the spark is to be poetry. Poetry becomes the instrument of redemption; it invades the territory of faith and sets up a succession of short-lived governments: while a horde of intrusive busybodies in the meantime invade its own domain. The generous confusion of the nineteenth century has begun.

NOTES

Chapter IV. Shelley

1. Hogg, *Life of Shelley*, ed. Humbert Wolfe (1933); 84-5.
2. Letter to Godwin, January 3rd, 1812.
3. *v.* Brailsford, *Shelley, Godwin and their Circle.*
4. "I am acquainted with a lady of considerable accomplishments, and the mother of a numerous family, whom the Christian religion has goaded to an incurable insanity. A parallel case is, I believe, within the experience of every physician." Note to *Queen Mab.*
5. Preface to *Prometheus Unbound.*
6. Mary Shelley, *Note on "Prometheus Unbound".*
7. The third act was finished in April, the fourth not added till November 1819.
8. *v.* Grabo, *A Newton among Poets.*
9. Whitehead, *Science and the Modern World*, p. 105.
10. "O world! O life! O time!"
11. To Jane: "The keen stars were twinkling".
12. *With a guitar, to Jane.*
13. N. I. White, *Shelley*, II, 630, note 35.

CHAPTER V

KEATS

1. The Realm of Flora

FOR all our tendency to couple them together, there was no such alliance between Keats and Shelley as there was between Wordsworth and Coleridge. Their qualities were antithetical but not complementary. Shelley was "much disposed to dissect or anatomize any trip or slip" in *Endymion*—or Keats thought he was: and Keats was inclined to deplore Shelley's dissipation of his powers on other objects than pure poetry. Keats writes to Shelley:

> "I received a copy of the *Cenci*. . . . There is only one part of it I am judge of—the poetry and dramatic effect, which by many spirits nowadays is considered the Mammon. A modern work, it is said, must have a purpose, which may be the God. An artist must serve Mammon; he must have 'self-concentration'—selfishness, perhaps. You, I am sure, will forgive me for sincerely remarking that you might curb your magnanimity, and be more of an artist, and load every rift of your subject with ore. The thought of such discipline must fall like cold chains upon you, who perhaps never sat with your wings furled for six months together.[1]

The letter reveals admiration but imperfect sympathy. Some of the reasons for this were irrelevant social ones; but the main reason is indicated above. Keats hardly shared at all in Shelley's political and social passions. He did not see the poet as the trumpet that sings to battle, or the unacknowledged legislator of the world. "An artist must serve Mammon"—that is, his own art rather than humanity: and Keats is, therefore, the first of those in the nineteenth century who wished to carve out a separate kingdom for the arts, and this letter perhaps

marks the beginning in England of the doctrine that was later to
develop into "Art for art's sake". However, it is only the beginning, and the development belongs to a later story. Keats is
never really happy in this belief and never works out its implications to his own satisfaction. Its significance for the study of
Keats himself is that it shows him as above all the conscious
artist, anxious to load his poetry as fully as possible with its own
special kind of excellence. We see the result of it in the devoted
critical care he gives to his own poetical development, the
constant effort to correct faults in technique and emotional
tone, to abandon harmful models and choose better ones, above
all to think out the essentials of his own kind of poetry to the
exclusion of everything else.

During his short career, therefore, Keats's work is always
changing and developing. At his death he seems to have been on
the edge of a further stage of growth. If Shelley had lived longer
there would have been more Shelley, but probably more of the
same kind. We feel of Keats that there was much to come that
would have been new and different. It is not much use to
speculate on the direction in which he would have moved.
There were so many conflicts unresolved at the time of his
death. The relation of art, his own kind of art, to human life as
a whole was a question that perplexed him from the beginning.
What he says to Shelley above can be countered, as we shall
see, by passages in which he implies the opposite—that the
"magnanimity" of sharing the distresses of humanity is
essential to the poet's growth. He lived in an age when a smack
of the philanthropist, the "friend to humanity", was expected of
liberal and enthusiastic youth; and he began his career in a
circle of liberal enthusiasts. Yet he cannot really worry himself
about many of the things that worried them; he feels obscurely
of a great liberal of the past that he was not quite a "friend to
humanity" in the contemporary sense, and we find him wonder-
ing "whether Milton's apparently less anxiety for Humanity
proceeds from his seeing farther or no than Wordsworth".[2]
He ultimately concludes that "a mighty providence subdues
the mightiest minds to the service of the time being".[3] But, we
might add, the whole tendency of Keats's work is to show that

Providence does not always do so in the most obvious way, that the artist does not necessarily proceed to the heart of humanity by the plainest and most-trodden route.

We must remember, too, what we all know, but perhaps without feeling it fully, that Keats's artistic intuition is far in advance of his ordinary experience—that at the time of his death the commonest problems of personal adjustment, even of a position in the world, were still, because of illness, because of poverty, not even on the way to a solution.

> His art is happy, but who knows his mind?
> I see a schoolboy when I think of him,
> With face and nose pressed to a sweet-shop window,
> For certainly he sank into his grave
> His senses and his heart unsatisfied,
> And made—being poor, ailing and ignorant
> Shut out from all the luxury of the world,
> The coarse-bred son of a livery-stable keeper—
> Luxuriant song.[4]

So Yeats wrote of him a hundred years later. Keats had far fewer advantages of circumstance than any other of the romantic poets. His passion for poetry began at school. A short attempt as a surgeon's apprentice was soon abandoned, and from then he devoted himself entirely to poetry. How he lived is somewhat of a mystery in these days when a poet's first duty is to find a steady job. But at that time even the arts seemed able to subsist in a precarious independence. His introduction to the literary world was through Leigh Hunt, a man to whom it is difficult to be fair. He was a sufficiently sincere political liberal to suffer for his beliefs, and a good minor essayist; but he was a poor minor poet, and an aesthete and professional beauty-lover of a particularly lax and tiresome kind. His was not an age or *milieu* with any great security of taste. The civilized decorum of the eighteenth century was departing and the Victorian moral responsibility had not arrived to take its place. It was under Hunt's auspices that Keats's first book of poems appeared in 1817.

It is full of echoes of his early poetical enthusiasms. Themes of romance and chivalry, derived mainly from Spenser, are found in *Calidore* and *Specimen of an Induction*; one of the poems is an avowed *Imitation of Spenser*; and a passion for Homer, known through the Elizabethan translation of Chapman, is recorded in the famous sonnet. It is often said that Keats, being ignorant of Greek, drew his knowledge of Greek myth and literature from Lempriere's Classical Dictionary: and no doubt Keats, like other boys, read his classical dictionary. His vision of Greece really came to him, however, through Elizabethan and seventeenth-century poetry, soaked like all Renaissance literature in Greek myth and allusions, yet luxuriant, disorderly and mediaevalized.[5] The country he was really exploring at this time was a legendary fairyland, and whether its ostensible situation was Hellas or Lyonnesse did not make much difference.

The imagery in detail, however, is not literary: it is drawn from a very minute and delicate sensuous observation. Keats, like Gautier, was "un homme pour qui le monde visible existe". And the visible world for Keats meant chiefly the world of nature; not nature with all the mystical and moral overtones that Wordsworth found in it, but simply the unanalysed delightfulness of living and growing things. It is the delicacy of the perception that strikes one first. There are many examples in *I stood tip-toe upon a little hill*, the first poem in the book.

> —the sweet buds which with a modest pride
> Pull droopingly, in slanting curve aside,
> Their scantly-leaved and finely-tapering stems.   (3)

> Here are sweet peas, on tip-toe for a flight
> With wings of gentle flush o'er delicate white,
> And taper fingers catching at all things,
> To bind them all about with tiny rings.   (57)

> Where swarms of minnows show their little heads,
> Staying their wavy bodies 'gainst the stream.   (72)

There is nothing here that could not be seen in a summer afternoon on Hampstead Heath, and, most happily, in all Keats's later excursions into the exotic and the remote, this delighted observation of familiar things is allowed its part. His dream-landscapes are always made up out of elements that are actual enough, not out of the starry and cloudy imaginings of Shelley. Nobody who could see actual things with this sort of fresh fineness could ever become entirely lost in luxuriant sentimentalizing; but the beauties of these poems are chiefly in fragments, and there are other fragments of a more unhappy kind.

The verses *On receiving a Curious Shell* and *A Copy of Verses from some Ladies* make one reflect that Keats would have been better off at this stage of his career without so many ladies, or with ladies of a different kind; and some of the familiar sonnets suggest a small and rather silly mutual admiration society. It is not only a question of technical immaturity, or even entirely of emotional immaturity, but of a sort of complacent *schwärmerei*, bred of

> the daily 'Tea is ready',
> Snug coterie and literary lady

that Byron so much detested.

> Give me a golden pen, and let me lean
> On heap'd up flowers, in regions clear and far;
> Bring me a tablet whiter than a star
> Or hand of hymning angel, when 'tis seen
> The silver strings of heavenly harp atween:
> And let there glide by many a pearly car
> Pink robes, and wavy hair, and diamond jar.[6]

This is almost worthy of glorious Technicolor; it is remarkable that a description of such concentrated vulgarity could be produced by the writer of the lines quoted earlier. And it turns out in the end that the occasion of these pantomime splendours is only that the poet has to go home early from a party.

It is customary to blame the badnesses of Keats's early verse on Hunt; but it is a rarely performed act of justice to see what Hunt's poetic vices really were and how far Keats borrowed them. *The Story of Rimini* was at this time Hunt's great claim to notice. It is a handling of the Paolo and Francesca

episode from Dante, debased to utter vulgarity by an affectation of colloquial ease and a sort of chatty pertness. He combines this with a cocky sniggering appreciation of feminine
charms. The verse, in deliberate reaction to the antithetic
regularity of the eighteenth-century couplet, is loose, the
sentences ambling easily from one couplet to another; and the
vocabulary is common and slovenly. All this is odd, for Hunt
wrote some excellent light verse, and was an Italian and Latin
scholar of some attainment: but there does seem to have been
an essential vulgarity of mind. Keats imitates the slipshod
neologisms, and sometimes the cosy familiarity with beauty of
the poetry-lover's circle: and a lip-smacking appreciation of
obvious sensuous charms. But the emotional tension of his
verse is far too high for him to follow the Cockney chattiness of
Hunt; and the sometimes excessive richness and luxuriance of
his early verse is not like Hunt at all.

The most important poem in the 1817 volume is *Sleep and
Poetry*. It is an early attempt to formulate his poetic ideals,
and is still written very much in the Huntian manner. (It was
actually composed in Hunt's house.) But it contains within itself
the reasons why this manner was not to satisfy Keats for long.
The central part of the poem describes prophetically what he
foresees to be his course in poetry.

> First the realm I'll pass
> Of Flora and old Pan: sleep in the grass
> Feed upon apples red and strawberries,
> And choose each pleasure that my fancy sees.   (101)

These lines and the twenty that follow describe a phase of
delighted communion with nature, and with all the external and
obvious beauties of the world. He wonders whether he can
ever bear to give up these sensuous ecstasies, but realizes in
the same breath that they are only a stage in his progress.

> And can I ever bid these joys farewell?
> Yes, I must pass them for a nobler life
> Where I may find the agonies, the strife
> Of human hearts.   (122)

A sort of vision follows, in which "shapes of delight, of mystery and fear" are seen, coming from the clouds and moving about the earth—symbolical of all the variety and passion of life, all that cannot be apprehended simply as sensuous beauty. This is the earliest statement of the problem that haunts Keats throughout his short life—the attempt to reconcile the loveliness of the world with its transience, its pleasures with its pain, the longing to enjoy the beautiful with the suspicion that it cannot be long enjoyed unless much that is not beautiful is faced. He was never to find a solution to these conflicts, and was never resigned as a modern poet might be, to write poetry of blank conflict: he was entering on a new phase of exploration when he died. The theme recurs in a letter of the next year to his friend Reynolds.

"Well, I compare human life to a large Mansion of Many Apartments, two of which I can only describe, the doors of the rest being as yet shut upon me. The first we step into we call the infant or thoughtless Chamber, in which we remain as long as we do not think. We remain there a long while, and notwithstanding the doors of the second Chamber remain wide open, showing a bright appearance, we care not to hasten into it; but are at length imperceptibly impelled by the awakening of the thinking principle within us—we no sooner get into the second chamber, which I shall call the Chamber of Maiden-Thought, than we become intoxicated with the light and atmosphere, we see nothing but pleasant wonders, and think of delaying there for ever in delight. However, among the effects this breathing is father of is that tremendous one of sharpening one's vision into the heart and nature of Man—of convincing one's nerves that the world is full of Misery and Heartbreak, Pain, Sickness and oppression—whereby this Chamber of Maiden-Thought becomes gradually darken'd and at the same time on all sides of it many doors are set open—but all dark—all leading to dark passages. . . . Now if we live, and go on thinking, we too shall explore them."[7]

But these utterances are yet largely prophetic, and Keats is

still in the realm of Flora, or the bright chamber of Maiden-
Thought. To return to *Sleep and Poetry*; the vision of his own
development is followed by a short essay in criticism, chiefly
interesting for showing the view of the history of English
poetry that prevailed in Hunt's circle. In former days the altar
of poetry "shone e'en in this isle"—presumably in Elizabethan
days. At that time "the Muses were nigh cloyed with honours":
but in the succeeding age all this was forgotten, and

>   a schism
> Nurtured by foppery and barbarism,
> Made great Apollo blush for this his land.
> Men were thought wise who could not understand
> His glories: with a puling infant's force
> They swayed about upon a rocking-horse
> And thought it Pegasus.   (182)

—the puling infants being, one supposes, Dryden and Pope,
and their exercises on the rocking horse the balanced antithetic
couplets in which, for instance, the portraits of Achitophel and
Sporus were written. As criticism this is little more than boyish
impertinence, but it shows how the dogma of romanticism was
already beginning to harden. The Augustan age already appears
as an unfortunate interregnum in the history of poetry; and this
becomes so much the established orthodoxy that fifty years later
Matthew Arnold, a critic of by no means exclusively romantic
leanings, can describe Dryden and Pope as "not classics of our
poetry, but classics of our prose", in the tone of one who is
saying what no one has ever doubted. Keats's attack is con-
ducted with considerable spirit, and with an energy of contempt that makes it almost worthy of the eighteenth century
itself: but the view of English poetic history is at least as partial
as that which, a hundred years earlier, would have informed us
that Mr. Denham and Mr. Waller were the first refiners of our
numbers, and that the sweetness of English verse was never
practised before the institution of their reforms.

The major fruit of this period of Keats's career is *Endymion*,
which appeared in the next year, in 1818. The preface, however,

shows that Keats was dissatisfied with it as soon as it was
finished, and that the dissatisfaction was not only with the technique, but with the general state of feeling in which it was
written.

"The imagination of a boy is healthy, and the mature
imagination of a man is healthy; but there is a space of life
between, in which the soul is in a ferment, the character
undecided, the way of life uncertain, the ambition thick-
sighted: thence proceed mawkishness, and all the thousand
bitters which those men I speak of must necessarily taste in
going over the following pages."

This is a surprising piece of self-criticism for a man of
twenty, and disarms in advance almost all that need be said on
the matter. The technical signs of the ferment and indecision
are chiefly in the handling of the long narrative. It is not that
the poem is without a plan—it started with a reasonably clear
one; but the transitions are not clearly made, so that it is often
difficult to tell what is happening; and the whole is desperately
obscured by a profusion of ornament. Keats cannot refrain
from chasing any descriptive butterfly that turns up, and the
reader finds it genuinely hard to follow him in his ramblings.
The classical "schism nurtured by foppery and barbarism" had
laid down rules for the conduct of an epic poem, and expected
any narrative poem to be planned with lucidity and logic.
Many of the rules were arbitrary; but it is unfortunate that
when they were thrown overboard the underlying ideal of
lucidity often went with them. Antipathy to the "rocking-
horse" rhythm of the eighteenth-century couplet was an article
of faith in the Hunt circle. This arose partly from blindness to
the real energy and variety of eighteenth-century verse, partly
from a perfectly just recognition that its bite and sharpness are
not the only effects of which the couplet is capable, and a
perfectly natural desire to aim at other sensations. *Endymion*
is therefore written in the loose Huntian couplet, and this
reinforces the effect of laxity produced by the structure.

The theme of the poem is one that is endemic in romantic

literature—the pursuit in the world of an ideal love who has been glimpsed dimly in vision. So far it is the same as that of Shelley's *Alastor*. Keats embodies it in a rehandling of the Greek fable of Diana's love for Endymion, a mortal shepherd: but he lays the emphasis on Endymion's love for Diana rather than on hers for him. The goddess visits Endymion in sleep, and when he awakes he resolves to seek her through the world. After numerous confusing adventures he meets an Indian maiden who is sad and homesick, lamenting a lost love. He is sorry for her, and because he is sorry for her comes to love her; and for a time he forgets his goddess. This seems an infidelity, but is not really so, for in the end Diana and the Indian maiden turn out to be the same. That is to say, ideal beauty can only be achieved by love and sympathy for the beauty immanent in human life. The conclusion is quite different from that of Alastor, who, not finding his veiled maid, can only die disappointed. Keats does not accept the blank Shelleyan dichotomy between the world of experience and the world of imagination. Endymion achieves his quest, but only by apparently compromising his love for a goddess by love for a mortal. Keats is recurring here to the idea we have met already in *Sleep and Poetry*, in the letter to Reynolds, and that we are to meet again in the second Hyperion; the idea that the love of beauty, like other passions, cannot exist fruitfully in isolation, that it can only fulfil itself through participation in the actual conditions of human life. Thus the leading idea of *Endymion* is not something mawkish or undecided, but a quite vigorous existentialist principle that Keats saw clearly from the beginning of his life. The trouble is that he sees it as a principle before he is able to grasp it in any concrete embodiment. Convinced that he must leave the joys of "the realm of Flora and old Pan" for "the agony and strife of human hearts", he still does not know how to do it. The descriptive passages are rich, luxuriant and fertile in invention, but uncertain in purpose. Sometimes they give the impression that he is perfectly content with this catalogue of "luxuries" (a favourite word with Keats at this time), and content to let it obscure the ground-plan of the work; at other times he seems to be chasing through all this loveliness of detail some other kind of loveliness that he is not yet able to grasp. And the presentation of emotion is sentimental and monotonous —simply because it is unrealized, because Keats has yet had little experience of the divagations of the heart, little time even to look into his own. Perhaps if he had had more he would have found that narrative poetry was not to be the medium in which he was really to express himself most fully.

The three short narratives *Lamia*, *Isabella* and *The Eve of St. Agnes* all belong to the volume of 1820 which also contained *Hyperion* and the Odes. *Isabella* was written immediately after the completion of *Endymion*, and belongs to the same emotional phase. Shortly after it was written the *Quarterly* published a contemptuously abusive review of *Endymion*, concentrating its fire on the style and diction, but more fundamentally offended by the sentiment. After this Keats hesitated for a time over the publication of *Isabella*. He was not, as is often said, particularly distressed by the rough handling he received. He describes *Isabella* as "a weak-sided poem, with an amusing sober-sadness about it"[8] and quite good-humouredly recognized that its adolescent sentiment lays it open to the same kind of crude man-of-the-world mockery as had greeted its predecessor. In one sense it attempts more than *Endymion*, for it tries to deal with grief and passionate love, even to some extent with character. Again we find Keats knowing the direction in which he wants to move before he is actually capable of taking the step. He wants to do something nearer to "breathing human passion" than the love of a mythical shepherd for a goddess, but as he says himself, "There is too much inexperience of life and simplicity of knowledge in it". The sweet and gentle sentiment of the poem is incongruous with the horrible theme, and slips easily into sentimentality. This results often in a weak luxuriance of diction:

> So said, his erewhile timid lips grew bold,
> And poesied with hers in dewy rhyme.

A tender prettiness is the note of the poem, which remains after all an incomplete attempt at exploring one of the passages leading out of the chamber of Maiden-Thought.

Lamia was written after the *Endymion* review, and is a conscious attempt at correcting its technical immaturities. So far from being "snuffed out by an article" Keats was set on by it to a sober attempt at technical improvement. Soon after the completion of *Endymion* Keats also experienced a revulsion against the taste of Hunt and his circle. "Hunt does one harm by making fine things petty and beautiful things hateful."[9] *Lamia* is accordingly written in a much tighter form of couplet, and a much clearer and less sprawling kind of narrative—both being derived perhaps from a study of Dryden, though the verse is not very like Dryden in detail. A rather unhappy attempt at easy, man-of-the-world cynicism in the tone is probably aimed at making the poem less obnoxious to hard-boiled *Quarterly* ridicule. Keats valued it as a break from the sentimental atmosphere of his earlier work, and there is some very fine verse in it; but it remains otherwise a rather purposeless poem, and it looks rather like an exercise in verse-narrative.

Any poet whose work is as continually progressive as that of Keats must make these tentative and unfulfilled explorations. His most completely successful short narrative poem is the one where he remains most completely within the range of decorative romantic experience. This is *The Eve of St. Agnes*. It was written in the first flush of his acquaintance with Fanny Brawne, before illness and, perhaps, her lack of real sympathy, had made the hope of an idyllic and happy love impossible for him. It is full of a dreamy sensuous happiness which finds its expression (and this is typical of Keats) in a rich decorative pattern rather than in any precise delineation of passion and sentiment. The poetic equivalent for an emotion with Keats is commonly a picture: what he has to say about feeling as such is often quite vague and generalized: even his rhythms are less acutely responsive to changes of emotional tone than those of many other poets: it is by the precision of his sensuous imagery —bright and clear, yet rich, like the figures in a painted missal —that he commands the response that he wants. This imagery is chiefly visual: (the clear pictorial quality explains his appeal to the pre-Raphaelite painters) but images of sound, of touch, even of taste, also play their part; and the reader who is content

to respond simply to the rich sensuous surface of such a poem
as *The Eve of St. Agnes* is in the end likely to understand Keats
better than one who is too addicted to philosophical short cuts.
The story is slight to the verge of insignificance, the setting is
romantic-mediaeval, from Mrs. Radcliffe, Chatterton and
Spenser; but all the senses are alert and their apprehensions
touched with the greatest precision and delicacy.

> The silver, snarling trumpets 'gan to chide
> > (iv)

> Out went the taper as she hurried in;
> Its little smoke, in pallid moonshine, died.
> > (xxiii)

> A casement high and triple-arched there was,
> All garlanded with carven imag'ries
> Of fruit, and flowers, and bunches of knot-grass,
> And diamonded with panes of quaint device.
> > (xxiv)

> The arras, rich with horseman, hawk and hound,
> Fluttered in the besieging wind's uproar:
> And the long carpets rose along the gusty floor.
> > (xl)

With our post-symbolist tastes we are too likely to be
unappreciative of this sort of descriptive writing, even while
we recognize its aptness. But we should be wrong to think of it
as *merely* "decorative". The idea of a lucky love triumphant
over obstacles could never express itself in Keats by the rhap-
sodic anatomizing of sentiment that we find in *Epipsychidion*:
this succession of clear, bright images of sight, sound and touch
is the only means by which his imaginative life can find its
incarnation. The fragment of *The Eve of St. Mark* has the
same quality—a fairy-tale theme and setting combined with
the most vivid and delicate realization of detail. Keats has been
reproved for wishing once for a life of sensations rather than of

thoughts: the key to his poetry is that most of the time his sensations were his thoughts, the kind of thought that could not be embodied in sensuous and pictorial form was hardly possible to him.

The lover in *The Eve of St. Agnes* wakened his Madeline by playing

> an ancient ditty long since mute
> In Provence called 'La Belle Dame sans Mercy'.

The name appears to have fascinated Keats, and not long afterwards he wrote the poem of that name. It is thus dramatically conceived, and springs out of the atmosphere of *The Eve of St. Agnes*. But it is a far less conscious poem, and springs perhaps from a different layer of the mind. La Belle Dame is the fatal woman-figure, like Circe or Tannhauser's Venus, who haunts romantic literature. She is the opposite of the pure and ideal Madeline, and yet the same person; one of the many forms the woman image assumes in the unconscious imagination. The imagery and phrasing have the perfect harmonious strangeness of a dream. If the essence of romantic poetry is to rely on sources of inspiration other than the rational intellect can supply, this poem may be justly considered its quintessence, and its hidden source is shown in the magical compulsive rhythm, less opulent and deliberate than is usual with Keats, more unexplainably haunting.

ii. 'NEGATIVE CAPABILITY'

So far, the most living thing in Keats's poetry has been the re-creation of sensuous beauty, first as a source of delight for its own sake, then as a symbol of the life of the mind and the emotions. Speculative and philosophical interests always formed the major part of Shelley's experience, and the young Wordsworth for a time was hag-ridden by them: there is almost no trace of this in Keats. The academic education which he never had tends to foster abstract thought; but Keats would never have lived by it whatever his training. He not only cared little for, but positively resented intellectual truths which make demands upon the mind without being verifiable in immediate experience. "Axioms in philosophy are not axioms until they are proved upon our pulses. We read fine things, but never feel them to the full till we have gone the same steps as the author."[10] Keats almost hates a writer who tries to force the world and the reader to his own conclusions, and at times he felt that Wordsworth did so. "For the sake of a few fine imaginative or domestic passages, are we to be bullied into a certain Philosophy engendered in the whims of an egotist. . . . We hate poetry that has a palpable design upon us."[11] Argument and dialectic seem to him an offensive self-assertion. "Man should not dispute or assert, but whisper results to his neighbour."[12] He distinguishes the poetical character to which he belongs from the "Wordsworthian or egotistical sublime": its essence is that

> "it has no self—it is everything and nothing—It has no character—it enjoys light and shade; it lives in gusto, be it foul or fair, high or low, rich or poor, mean or elevated—It has as much delight in conceiving an Iago as an Imogen. What shocks the virtuous philosopher delights the camelion Poet."[13]

For Keats, the necessary precondition of poetry is submission to things as they are, without trying to intellectualize them into something else, submission to people as they are, without trying to indoctrinate or improve them. (We meet all this again, developed into a whole poetical creed, in Yeats's early essays.) Keats found this quality at its fullest in Shakespeare.

> "It struck me what quality went to form a man of achievement, especially in literature—I mean *Negative Capability*, that is, when a man is capable of being in uncertainties, mysteries, doubts, without any irritable reaching after fact and reason."[14]

This way of feeling grows naturally into a strong active and dramatic tendency, a wish to participate in the life of others, and an understanding of other people that is everywhere evident in the letters. Often Keats feels that this participation in the life of others, "the agony and strife of human hearts", ought to be the mainspring of his poetry. But it is not. The dealings with character and emotion are not the most memorable things in Keats's poetry. There are natures whose passion for life includes, but goes beyond, personality. D. H. Lawrence was perhaps one of these, and there is something of it in Keats. The total impression of the moment, the fusion of his own subjective emotion with sensations from the outside world is the ultimate reality for him; and the most typical and individual remarks in the letters seem to be in passages like the following:

"I scarcely remember counting upon any Happiness— I look not for it if it be not in the present hour—nothing startles me beyond the Moment. The setting sun will always set me to rights—or if a sparrow comes before my window I take part in its existence and pick about the Gravel."[15]

Such a nature is not likely to find its best expression in a narrative of character and events, (or, as Keats hoped, in drama). It is at its height in moments of impassioned contemplation, when the life of the spirit is closely bound up with the objects of immediate sensuous experience. It was in some such mood that the *Ode on Indolence* was written. It is the first of the great Odes, written in March 1819; and all of them were written in this year. In the *Ode on Indolence* not Love, nor Ambition, nor Poetry makes it worth while to give up the luxurious enjoyment of the moment: none of them is

> so sweet as drowsy noons
> And evenings steep'd in honied indolence;
> O, for an age so sheltered from annoy,
> That I may never know how change the moons,
> Or hear the voice of busy common-sense!

Lines which might have served Matthew Arnold as the text for his sermon on Keats, the relaxed and sensuous man.

"But what shocks the virtuous philosopher delights the camelion Poet."

> My soul had been a lawn besprinkled o'er
> With flowers, and stirring shades, and baffled beams:
> The morn was clouded, but no shower fell,
> Tho' in her lids hung the sweet tears of May;
> The open casement pressed a new-leaved vine,
> Let in the budding warmth and throstle's lay;

It is all exquisite and all utterly transitory; and out of the knowledge of this is born a longing for a world in which such moments could become eternal. All the Odes are closely bound up with this theme of transience and permanency. Yeats, on the same theme, wrote simply

> Man is in love, and loves what vanishes.
> What is there more to say?

Keats is not capable of this sort of twentieth-century stoicism; he must attempt to reconcile the contradiction. Perhaps this is one of the differences between classical and romantic poetry. It is the classical poet who accepts with resignation the passing of earthly joys and is, therefore, free to gather his rose-buds while he may (Yeats is writing above in an untypically neo-classic moment); the romantic poet tries desperately to find some permanent and unchanging refuge in a world of flux, longing for an age in which he may never know the moon's changes, or for a shadowy isle of bliss where he can forget the beating of the steely sea. Thus for the romantic there is always the element of conflict, either in the poetry, itself or just outside it; and since he is asking questions to which there is no answer, he is little likely to reach a serene conclusion. The best he can do is to find a way of facing a contradiction whose intensity he refuses to minimize; and this is better than saying you don't believe in ghosts while there is one breathing down your neck.

The *Ode to Psyche* seems the farthest away from all this, the most purely fanciful. It would be easy to take it as a piece of lovely decorative mythology: but it is probably something more. Psyche is the soul, not recognized as a goddess in the classic Greek mythology. But neither is she the soul in the Christian sense. The absence of any specifically Christian feeling, indeed of any kind of orientation to Christianity, is remarkable in Keats. His main religious feeling is a longing, perfectly expressed in the fourth stanza of this ode, for the natural piety of antiquity

> When holy were the haunted forest boughs,
> Holy the air, the water and the fire.

Yet Keats still makes the practical distinction between what is believed and what is merely imagined, and is quite unable to attempt to *believe* in nature-spirits or Olympus' faded hierarchy. Psyche, the last addition to the ancient pantheon, never formally worshipped in the ancient world, is the only one of the old deities who is still real.

> Yet even in these days so far retired
> From happy pieties, thy lucent fans
> Fluttering among the faint Olympians
> I see, and sing, by my own eyes inspired.

So the last stanza with its promise to

> be thy priest, and build a fane
> In some untrodden region of my mind,

with its lovely, half-inspired, half-natural imagery, is not merely a piece of fanciful devotion to an obsolete myth; but a recognition by Keats that his own exploration is to be of the interior landscape, that his ultimate devotion is to be neither to the objective world, nor to any power outside himself.

Indolence records a moment when sensuous happiness is complete and sufficient and its own justification. The trouble with such experiences, as the poem implicitly recognizes, is that they are only momentary. To Keats, with his appetite for the immediately experienced, they are the most real and important things in life. "We become intoxicated with the light and the atmosphere" of such moments: but among the effects they give rise to is that "of convincing one's nerves that the world is full of Misery and Heartbreak, Pain, Sickness and Oppression". At the time he wrote the *Ode to a Nightingale*, Keats needed little reminding of this. It was only a few months after the death of his brother Tom from a painful and distressing illness, and the memory of this is in the third stanza. The poem is not, as is sometimes said, a contrast between his own despondency and the happiness of the bird. It is about the contrast between his own immediately experienced happiness in the bird's song, his imaginative participation in an untroubled natural life, and a less immediate but more enduring knowledge of sorrow. Happiness is momentary and transient: the only thing certain is

> The weariness, the fever and the fret
> Here, where men sit and hear each other groan;
> Where palsy shakes a few, sad, last grey hairs,
> Where youth grows pale, and spectre-thin, and dies,
> Where but to think is to be full of sorrow
>   And leaden-eyed despairs.

The heart-ache and the drowsy numbness of the opening lines do not describe mere dejection, but a sort of drugged state, which can only be maintained by further intoxication (Stanza 2). Wine is the traditional soother of men's cares, the traditional means of prolonging a drowsy sensuous enjoyment; and Keats sometimes said he enjoyed claret. But though he had his Anacreontic intervals, they are no real answer for him, and in the fourth stanza he realizes that the only way of escaping to share the happiness of the bird is "on the viewless wings of Poesy". Poetry means first of all imagination—imaginative participation in the bird's life: secondly, it means the actual poetry he is writing—the incantatory loveliness of the fourth and fifth stanzas does make this moment permanent, in a sense: but not in the sense that Keats the living and suffering human being really desires. The only way in which it can really be made eternal is to die at the moment of greatest sensuous happiness. "I have been half in love with easeful death." Much ink has been spilt on the romantic poets' pursuit of death. "Keats's longing for death and his mother has become a by-word among the learned" (W. Empson). Maybe it has; but like the Freudian death-wish which has also become a by-word, it does not mean what is most obvious on the surface. The Freudian death-wish is the desire of the cell to resist the encroachments of outside experience, to remain enclosed in its own kind of contentment. So the romantic poet's desire for death is not a longing for extinction, it is the desire to make a happiness that he knows to be transient last for ever. And Keats is only half in love with easeful death—the other half of his consciousness knows well enough that this answer is only the negation of any possible answer. But art offers a type of permanence; and by a startling transformation in the seventh stanza the nightingale becomes a symbol of the artist and its song a symbol of art.

It has often been said that this is an audacious paradox, that the nightingale, so far from being immortal, has a considerably shorter life than man, and that its song is only immortal in the sense that through history there have always been nightingales' songs and that they have always had the same power of enchantment. But it is only in this sense that immortality can be predicated of poets; in fact, the poet's position is stronger, for his individual song endures. There is, therefore, no breach in the poetic logic. But the argument is a casuistry none the less, because the special case of poetic immortality is used, or is on the point of being used, as if it offered the kind of enduring happiness that Keats seeks as a man. But it does not, and cannot do so. (It is small consolation to the sorrows of Eohippus, as T. H. Huxley once remarked, that one of his remote descendants is some day to win the Derby.) So the last word of the seventh stanza, "forlorn", recalls Keats the poet who creates, foreseeing a poetic immortality, to Keats the man who suffers, foreseeing only sickness and sorrow and an early death. The song of the nightingale fades, and Keats finishes where, unlike Shelley, he generally finishes, with his feet on the ground. On the level of ordinary human experience there is no solution to the conflict. The poet who creates can offer little consolation to the man who suffers: but on the level of poetic creation the conflict disappears. Transitory human happiness is given permanence in a different sense by being embodied in art.

The *Ode on a Grecian Urn* takes up the thought of the seventh stanza of the *Ode to a Nightingale*. De Selincourt suggests as its motto a phrase of Leonardo's: *Cosa bella mortal passa e non d'arte*—Mortal beauties pass away, but not those of art. It is a much more objective and descriptive poem than the *Nightingale*. It is too often forgotten that Keats's imaginative glimpse of Greece was derived not only from translated literary sources, but also from actual Greek plastic art, and that he had had more chance of experiencing it at first hand than earlier and more learned neo-classical connoisseurs; for the Elgin marbles had been recently acquired by the British Museum, and Keats had been profoundly impressed by them. Indeed the imagery of the ode seems to have been suggested more by these sculptures than by any individual vase-painting. The urn is taken as a type of enduring beauty; and again the immortality of art is only a quasi-immortality; for though ceramics last longer than most things they are not in any metaphysical sense more indestructible than mere human clay. There is no real analogy between the loves and pastoral felicities on the urn and "breathing human passion"; the contrast between the permanence of the one and the transience of the other is another poetic casuistry. But this time it is directed to a different end. The poet's momentary emotional state enters less into the poem. He is concerned to establish at least one enduring value below the sphere of the moon, and he finds it in the existence of the beauty of art. It is the only way in which human feeling and natural loveliness can be given lasting significance. The happy boughs that cannot shed their leaves and the lover who can never kiss, but whose love can never fade, are types of the only earthly paradise that exists; and the fact that it is not quite of the kind that men are looking for is not now in the foreground of consciousness.

The last two lines of the poem have been much discussed.

That beauty is truth, truth beauty is not all that we know on earth, and certainly not all that we need to know. In the days when it was the custom to take romantic modes of expression simply at their face value these lines were often read as the expression of a profound philosophy. Dr. Richards has taught his disciples to laugh at this reading of them, that the statement is conceptually meaningless and is only there for its value in communicating and organizing emotion. Neither of these views is particularly helpful. The lines must be read in their context, and in the context of the other odes. They are of course in the first place the expression of a moment of rapturous recognition of a beautiful object, and so far are equivalent to an exclamation of joy and reverence. But the sensuous resources of Keats's verse are so rich that he has no need to disguise his emotions of this kind as philosophical statements, unless he also means them in some sense to be so. And he says the same thing in prose: "I never can feel certain of any truth, but from a clear perception of its Beauty".[16] In this context, where transience and permanence are the two poles of the argument, "truth" means "that which has lasting value".[17] (The truth is great *and shall prevail*. What is true all the week is "truer" than what is true only on Monday morning.) Keats is saying that beauty is "truer" than love, pleasure and other forms of value, because they pass away while beauty can be embodied in a lasting quasi-permanent form. When poets say "ye" they are often addressing themselves or other poets. That beauty is truth and truth beauty is all that the artist, as artist, knows, and all he needs to know for the practice of his art.

> *Tout passe: l'art robuste*
> *Seule à l'éternité.*

Again, Keats finds a solution to his conflict valid for the artist, but leaving the suffering and experiencing man exactly where he was.

In the *Ode on Melancholy* and the *Ode to Autumn*, the problems of the artist are in abeyance, and Keats returns to ordinary human experience, to the problem of happiness in life.

The *Ode on Melancholy* recognizes that sadness is the inevitable complement of the moments of intense sensuous happiness that so far have been the peaks of his experience.

> She dwells with Beauty—Beauty that must die,
> And Joy, whose hand is ever at his lips,
> Bidding adieu.

It is therefore as vain to attempt to escape from this inevitable pain as to expect a light not to cast shadows. Melancholy springs from the transience of joy, and the transience of joy is a part of its nature. But the note of the poem is not that of *Carpe diem*, or *Gather ye rosebuds while ye may*. They suggest an eager grasping at pleasures that are soon to be snatched away. The whole movement and vocabulary of the Odes suggest a rich, slow brooding over beauty and joy, with a full realization both of beauty and the pain that its disappearance will bring, but with an enjoyment of such intensity and depth that it makes the moment eternal, in quality if not in duration.

The *Ode to Autumn* is pre-eminently the record of such an experience. It is in a sense a return to the mood of the *Ode on Indolence*—making the moment sufficient to itself. It is the most perfect in form and detail of the Odes, and also the most difficult to penetrate below the surface, for it is apparently the most purely objective and descriptive. The emotion has become completely fused with the object, and expresses itself completely through it. There are no questions and no conflict in the poem: the season of ripeness and fulfilment is seen as though it is quite final. Autumn as a poetical symbol is commonly the prelude to winter. Keats sees it as a still pause in time, when everything has reached fruition and ripeness is all. The old question almost raises its head in the last stanza:

> Where are the songs of spring? Ay, where are they?
> Think not of them, thou hast thy music too.

But it is immediately stilled, and the poem ends with the quiet relapse of consciousness into the soft natural loveliness that surrounds it.

It would be idle to try to turn the Odes into great philosophical poems. They come to no conclusion and make no
synthesis. Keats does not wholly avoid confusion between
permanent value and *value permanently accessible to the individual.*
His temperament, with its eager love of life, would have been
satisfied with a speculative solution like Yeats's belief in re-
incarnation: but he would surely have dismissed it as too fantastic: or like that of Mr. Dunne, whose New Immortality, if I
have not misunderstood it, suggests that after death a kind of
consciousness persists, that is in permanent possession of its
past experience.

> These metaphysics of magicians
> And necromantic books are heavenly.

But theirs was not the kind of speculation to which Keats was
prone. Yet the Odes are not merely decorative and descriptive
poems, as parts of them appear to be; nor yet poems of luxurious
self-abandonment; nor yet mere manipulations of feeling. The
deep conflict from which they spring is both emotional and
intellectual; yet they proceed solely by the methods peculiar to
poetry, not by the aid of the speculative intelligence. They are
in fact supreme examples of Negative Capability, "when a man
is capable of being in uncertainties, mysteries, doubts, without
any irritable reaching after fact and reason".

Keats found his real medium here, far more than in the
narrative poems. They are the summit of his achievement, for
Hyperion was only the beginning of a phase that he did not live
to complete. More than any other poet of his age he had the
power of externalizing his experience, of finding adequate
outward symbols for his experiences, instead of merely talking about them. This does not necessarily mean that he had
the dramatic gift: indeed, his knowledge of human character
and actions had hardly gone far enough for this to be possible.
Sensuous beauty and meditation on sensuous beauty was the
central experience of his life. It is in the Odes that he explores
this most fully, and perhaps for the time exhausts it. It is not
likely that he would have rested in this phase. Fighting against

it all the time was the active and dramatic tendency we have noticed above, the desire to make "the agony and strife of human hearts" the material of his verse. We must trace his further movement in this direction in the two versions of *Hyperion*.

iii. THE TWO HYPERIONS

Hyperion exists in two versions, the second being a revision of the first, with the addition of a long induction in a new style which makes it into a different poem. The chronology of the composition is obscure, since it was contemplated long before it was begun. Keats worked on it at intervals, and neither he nor his correspondents distinguish between the two versions in their letters. Without discussing the evidence in detail, for which the reader must be referred elsewhere,[18] we may say that the first version was written mostly before the great odes, the second mostly after them; and that the two extend, on and off, over Keats's greatest creative period, until increasing illness and despair finally made it impossible for him to work at all.

After the publication of *Endymion*, in 1818, Keats went on a summer tour in Scotland, during which he studied Dante, and severely injured his health by exposure. He returned to nurse his brother through his last illness, it was apparently during this period, in September, that *Hyperion* was begun. About the same time, Keats first met Fanny Brawne, with whom he was soon to be so hopelessly and disastrously in love; and he composed *The Eve of St. Agnes* in the first flush of new emotion. Work on *Hyperion*, therefore, cannot have been continuous. But by April 1819 the complete MS (or all there is of it, for the poem is a fragment) was in the hands of Woodhouse, literary adviser to Keats's publishers. The Odes and *La Belle Dame* occupy the next two months; and in the later summer Keats took up the poem again, presumably at work on the second version. In September, the month in which the *Ode to Autumn* was written, he writes that he has given *Hyperion* up; though he appears actually to have worked further on it in the winter of

1819, when his love for Fanny, increasing in intensity as it was frustrated by illness, was gradually wearing him out. The period covered by *Hyperion*, then, is the period of Keats's most intense experience, both of joy and sorrow, in actual life; and of his most rapid development: and it is not surprising, therefore, that the second version shows great changes from the first.

The idea of another poem on a mythological theme was in Keats's mind before he had finished *Endymion*, and he soon decided on the subject, the Fall of Hyperion. The theme of the war between the Titans, or earlier generation of gods, and the later Olympians who dispossessed them is often referred to in Keats's favourite literature, and he could have found the outlines of his story without referring to Lempriere for aid. The specific theme, the supplanting of Hyperion the old sun-god by Apollo the new, is Keats's own. Apollo is also the god of poetry, and as *Endymion* had symbolized the fate of the lover of beauty in the world, so the story of Apollo and Hyperion was perhaps going to symbolize the fate of the poet as creator. Since the poem is unfinished, we cannot know. What is immediately clear is how much the design owes to Milton. The poem opens in the regular epic manner, in the middle of the story. We find the Titans, like Milton's fallen angels, already outcast and shorn of their power. Hyperion alone is not yet overthrown, and, like Milton's Satan, he is the one hope of further resistance. The opening scene is followed by a council to discuss the regaining of the lost dominions, in which Enceladus, like Moloch, pronounces his sentence for open war, and Oceanus, like Belial, stands for more moderate measures. Externally, at least, this is modelled on *Paradise Lost*, and marks a clear break with the meandering structure of *Endymion*. The first two books look like the opening of an epic, and it seems that Keats's original design (we are told so by Woodhouse and the publishers[19]) was a poem of epic scope, in which the war in heaven would have been narrated, as in *Paradise Lost*, in the form of an episode. But it seems likely (and the more likely from the desultory composition of the work) that the plan changed, and that the two books we have are not a fragment of what should have been ten, but of a more contracted design. Definite evidence is wanting, and the situation must remain obscure. We cannot avoid speculation, however: in spite of its fragmentary condition, *Hyperion* remains Keats's most imposing piece of work, and the student of Keats must wish to know both why it was discontinued and how it would have gone on.

The publishers tell us that the reception of *Endymion* discouraged the author from proceeding. But this is untrue, and we have the evidence of chronology and a note from Keats himself to prove it.[19] Keats said that he gave it up because of the excessive Miltonism of the style[20]—but he says it almost casually in a passage where he is discussing other things; and there is not the slightest need to suppose that this was the only reason, or even the most important. Let us look at the poem as it stands.

The first book gives us a picture of the fallen Titans, with Saturn as the central figure, but Hyperion as the only one who remains even potentially active. The second book shows them in council, and the vital part of it is undoubtedly the speech of Oceanus. It is here that we begin to see the poem in a new perspective. The burden of his speech is as follows:

> My voice is not a bellows unto ire,
> Yet listen, ye who will, whilst I bring proof
> How ye, perforce, must be content to stoop:
> And in this proof much comfort will I give,
> If ye will take that comfort in its truth.
> We fall by course of Nature's law, not force
> Of thunder, or of Jove.   (II, 176)

Saturn was not the first power in the universe, and cannot expect to be the last. Chaos and darkness produced light; light brought heaven and earth and life itself into being, and the Titans were the first-born of life. Heaven and Earth are more beautiful than chaos and darkness:

> So on our heels a fresh perfection treads,
> A power more strong in beauty, born of us
> And fated to excel us.   (II, 212)

The Titans are not to repine or envy their successors:

> for 'tis the eternal law
> That first in beauty shall be first in might.

(II, 228)

The simple Clymene follows and confirms Oceanus by testifying to the beauty of the young Apollo's music, which she has heard. What does this mean for the poem as a whole? It means that Hyperion is not after all to be a poem of epic conflict in the old sense—it is to be a poem of evolution, of the supersession of lower forms by higher; and the successors are to prevail because they are superior in beauty.

In the fragment of Book III the interest shifts from the Titans to the young Apollo. Mnemosyne (Memory) alone among the Titans has formed relations with the younger gods. She has watched over the childhood of Apollo, and now she finds him wavering and uncertain of his course. In speech with her he finds the consciousness of his destiny and assumes his new-found godhead. At this point, the poem breaks off.

What has happened? It seems that what began as an epic poem about a mythological conflict has become a symbolical poem of a different kind. But in the process new difficulties have arisen. The conventional epic conflict would have afforded a wealth of scenes and incidents, outlined in Woodhouse's sketch of the proposed development of the poem.[21] The new scheme, of an evolution in beauty, presents far greater problems. It could hardly be embodied in events and actions, and would, therefore, not afford material for anything like the ten books originally proposed. Perhaps there were other difficulties as well. We have seen repeated evidence of a conflict in Keats's life between the longing for a state of changeless happiness—

> That I may never know how change the moons—

and on the other hand an urgent sense of the necessity for change and development, the necessity to emerge from the chamber of Maiden-Thought. But it is one thing to realize the need for change, quite another thing to effect it. We are perpetually finding that a certain kind of experience is exhausted, or about to be exhausted, without knowing what is to take its place. We are on the threshold of a new development, but the door is still shut. So it is with Keats. The thing that had been most real to him up to now was an impassioned sensuous contemplation, enjoyed in self-contained, timeless moments; and the longing to make them eternal. He can talk about leaving the realm of Flora, but he does not know the way out. He knows intellectually that the kind of beauty he has lived with up to now must be superseded by another kind—

> Shapes of delight and mystery and fear—

But he can only see it in uncertain glimpses. So, faced with his poem about development and change, he can take us to the threshold of the new life, but he can go no further. And he is not happy with such a theme, for his deepest experience up to now has been of states that seem, while they last, to be timeless. The young Apollo assumes his god-like knowledge, and his mind is filled with

> Names, deeds, gray legends, dire events, rebellions,
> Majesties, sovran voices, agonies,
> Creations and destroyings.   (III, 114)

But in Keats's own mind this knowledge is only potential; he is not yet in secure possession of it. And the poem remains unfinished because he does not know how it is to go on.[22]

When he comes to revise it he knows no more than before how it is to go on. So *Hyperion* as it stands is not continued: the second version ends as the first did. But he adds to it an induction, making his ultimate purpose clearer. He cannot finish the poem, but he can show the direction in which it was to move. He does not do this by describing a distantly seen goal. Truths were not truths to Keats till they were proved upon the pulses, and he works now as ever, by giving poetic embodiment to the actual state of his mind. The new induction is one of the most remarkable pieces of writing in Keats's work, and it is the beginning of a development of which he was not to see the end. However, we cannot appreciate it fully without some further examination of the technique of the poem.

The Miltonic influence is as obvious in the verse and diction of the first *Hyperion* as it is in the design. Keats had been "feasting upon" Milton in April 1818,[23] shortly after the completion of *Endymion*, and the influence, mingled attraction and repulsion, goes on intermittently for the next eighteen months, On the Scotch tour, immediately before the writing of *Hyperion*, he studied Dante in Cary's translation. Thus he came under the spell of two austerer masters in poetry than any he had known before. If there is anything Dantesque in *Hyperion*, it is in the later rather than the earlier version; but perhaps the remote effect of a reading of Dante can be seen throughout in the greater clarity and definiteness of the pictures. Keats was by now in strong revulsion from the bathos and vulgarity of the Huntian manner, and it is natural, therefore that he should turn to Milton, the obvious master of a style of assured and conscious grandeur—above all, of an *imitable* style. It is relatively easy, as the history of blank verse since the seventeenth century shows, to achieve something of Milton's dignity by imitating his verbal habits; and this Keats does. There is no need to exemplify the Miltonic echoes in detail. The most careless reader can hardly help noticing the constant use of inversions ("stride colossal", "rest divine") typical of Milton's Latinized style, but not so far much used by Keats. Especially noticeable is the trick of sandwiching a noun between two adjectives ("gold clouds metropolitan"). There are other fragments of classical sentence-structure too:

> save what solemn tubes,
> Blown by the serious Zephyrs, gave of sweet
> And wandering sounds.   (I, 206)

And a passage such as the following leaves us in no doubt of its provenance:

> So ended Saturn; and the God of the Sea,
> Sophist and sage from no Athenian grove,
> But cogitation in his watery shades,
> Arose, with locks not oozy, and began.   (II, 167)

Yet the Miltonisms are detachable, not organic: the basis of the verse is not Miltonic: it is still the verse of Keats, but immensely purged and strengthened by contact with a severer master. Some of the most beautiful images in their delicacy and precision are utterly unlike Milton's generalized verbal grandeur, and indeed could be by nobody but Keats.

> No stir of air was there
> Not so much life as on a summer's day
> Robs not one light seed from the feathered grass,
> But where the dead leaf fell, there did it rest.
>
> (I, 7)

The Miltonisms of the style seem to have been a worry to Keats. In one of the letters, after praising Chatterton, rather oddly, as "the purest writer in the English language", he goes on to say, "I have given up *Hyperion*—there were too many Miltonic inversions in it—Miltonic verse cannot be written but in an artful, or rather artist's humour. I wish to give myself up to other sensations. English ought to be kept up".[24] But the discomfort of the Miltonic externals is more than compensated in other directions.

The imagery and description are shorn of redundancies, and are far finer for being kept within bounds: and there is an enormous gain of dignity and force in the presentation of emotion. Indeed, *Hyperion* is Keats's most serious and considerable essay in the dramatic presentation of emotion—for the Titans are conceived in human terms, and their sorrows are human sorrows. There is far greater power, too, of discourse, of argument in verse, than ever before: there is no parallel in the earlier work to the speech of Oceanus; and Keats seems to be discovering, as Yeats did later, how useful this sheer rhetorical power can be, even to a poet whose aims are normally in another direction.

That part of the second *Hyperion* which is merely a re-handling of the first does not present any very profound changes, though they are fairly numerous. They are mostly in the direction of removing Miltonisms and other dispensable ornaments. Keats sacrifices some of his best lines in the process, and though he evidently wanted the greater bareness of style to fit in with that of the new opening, we mostly feel that the sacrifice is too great. This accounts for the myth that he undertook the revision of the poem in the decline of his powers. But it is hard to see how any one can have believed this on reading the new induction. After the Odes, it is surely Keats's greatest verse; and it is so in an entirely new way. There is nothing like the first three hundred lines of the new *Hyperion* in Keats's earlier work, and I know of nothing like it in English blank verse at all. The new notes in blank verse since Milton are not very numerous: there are innumerable Miltonics; there are the vital but rather graceless colloquial rhythms of Browning, and the almost too professional mellifluousness of Tennyson. This is different from any. The rapidity and directness remind one of Dante—though whether the Dantesque influence or Jacobean blank verse is really at work is hard to say. Both in reflective and descriptive passages the verse seems to stride instead of to linger, as Keats's verse has mostly done hitherto. And the new-found decision of style reflects a new decision, in the handling of ideas.

The second *Hyperion* is cast in the form of a dream, and the added opening describes this dream and its setting. It begins with a short prologue which affords an excellent example of the new tense and muscular verse.

> Fanatics have their dreams, wherewith they weave
> A paradise for a sect; the savage, too,
> From forth the loftiest fashion of his sleep
> Guesses at heaven; pity these have not
> Traced upon vellum or wild Indian leaf
> The shadows of melodious utterance.
> But bare of laurel they live, dream, and die;
> For poesy alone can tell her dreams;
> With the fine spell of words alone can save
> Imagination from the sable chain
> And dumb enchantment. Who alive can say,
> "Thou art no poet, may'st not tell thy dreams?"

> Since every man whose soul is not a clod
> Hath visions and would speak, if he had lov'd,
> And been well nurtured in his mother tongue.
> Whether the dream now purposed to rehearse
> Be poet's or fanatic's will be known
> When this warm scribe, my hand, is in the grave.

This is an attempt to define the position of poetry. The poet has his dreams in common with other men, but he alone is able to secure them from oblivion. (Again, the thought of the *Ode to a Grecian Urn*—only art can endure.) And the poet's dream differs from the fanatic's, because it is for the world, the fanatic's only for a sect. We pass on to the dream itself, which begins in a wood—not a wild and gloomy one like Dante's, but a pastoral scene with a meal of fruits set out, of which the poet eats, then drinks from a cool vessel of transparent juice. He falls into a deep sleep and awakes to find that the scene is changed, that he is in a vast shrine, at the western end of which are steps leading up to an altar, with a gigantic image and a priestess ministering to the sacred flame. As he approaches, the veiled priestess addresses him:

> If thou canst not ascend
> These steps, die on the marble where thou art.
>
> (I, 107)

A stifling numbness overcomes him, and he is unable to move; then new life is poured into him; he draws nearer to the altar and asks the priestess to explain the mysteries.

> None can usurp this height, returned that shade,
> But those to whom the miseries of the world
> Are misery, and will not let them rest.
> All else, who find a haven in the world
> Where they may thoughtless sleep away their days,
> If by chance into this fane they come,
> Rot on the pavement where thou rotted'st half.
>
> (I, 147)

This is the theme, already familiar in *Sleep and Poetry* and
in the letters—that the poet must not rest in poetical dreams
but must share the sorrows of humanity. In the following lines,
it is carried further. The actively virtuous are not to be found
in the shrine—they are working in the world. The poet is here
because of his weakness, because he is a dreamer, and is
afforded this one chance to save himself. An obscure passage
follows (I, 187–210), possibly meant for deletion, since a few
lines of it are repeated later on; yet apparently necessary to
complete the idea.[25] In it the prophetess qualifies her con-
demnation of "the dreamer tribe", and distinguishes further
between the poet and the mere dreamer:

> The one pours out a balm upon the world,
> The other vexes it.

She then reveals that the temple is Saturn's, the only
remaining shrine of the old gods, and she is Moneta, the sole
remaining priestess. Moneta is the Latin name of Mnemosyne,
who occurs, of course, in the Hyperion story itself. She is, as it
were, another avatar of Mnemosyne, performing the same
function for Keats as Mnemosyne had done for Apollo. Then
Moneta unveils herself, and is described, in verse of a sere,
burnt-out splendour that exceeds anything else in Keats.

> Then I saw a wan face,
> Not pined by human sorrows, but bright-blanch'd
> By an immortal sickness which kills not;
> It works a constant change, which happy death
> Can put no end to; deathwards progressing
> To no death was that visage; it had past
> The lily and the snow; and beyond these
> I must not think now, though I saw that face.
> But for her eyes I should have fled away.   (I, 256)

The poet asks to be shown the hidden story that lies behind the
survival of the mysterious temple: she consents to reveal it to
him—and the story of Hyperion and the Titans, much as we
had it before, then begins.

This is Keats's last attempt to define the place of the poet in the world. It is not an exaltation of the poet, like Shelley's *Defence*. The poet is less than the man of active virtue, and Keats is still absorbed by the contrast between the realm of Flora and the other kingdom that he suspects to lie beyond it. He has still not crossed the boundary, but he knows more of what to expect on the journey. It is notable how much of Keats's poetry is about poetry, its function, its glories and its limitations. It is as though he is perpetually trying to find a bridge between art and life, but is perpetually led back to art itself. Perhaps the solution for the artist is not to try to escape from the domain of art, but to explore it more closely. In *Hyperion*, as always, Keats makes no attempt to march straight forward to an intellectual conclusion; he shows us the steps and stairs of the mind by which a yet unseen conclusion may be reached. And he draws two distinctions—one between the practical and the visionary mind; and one between the creative visionary, the poet, and the mere dreamer who "vexes" the world with visions that he can do nothing to transmute into reality. At this point, Keats's experience stops; and disease and an unhappy love were to cut short the possibility of further exploration.

He wrote little after this: the *Ode to Autumn* was composed towards the end of 1819; in 1820 he seems to have written almost nothing, except the pathetic "Bright star" sonnet, written into a blank leaf of Shakespeare's poems on the eve of his departure for Italy. Among the fragments of his verse were found these terrible lines, probably addressed to Fanny Brawne.

> This living hand, now warm and capable
> Of earnest grasping, would, if it were cold
> And in the icy silence of the tomb,
> So haunt thy days and chill thy dreaming nights
> That thou wouldst wish thine own heart dry of blood
> So in my veins red life might stream again,
> And thou be conscience-calmed—see here it is—
> I hold it towards you.

This seems to be the solitary outcrop of a reef that otherwise runs underground; it reveals an intensity and dramatic force that is like that of a Jacobean tragedy—but not like anything else in Keats. It is possible that he reached his full maturity in this dark period when he had not power to express it. Perhaps this new-found power would actually have led to drama. This is what Keats hoped himself; we find him talking, late in 1819, of "the writing of a few fine plays"[26] as his greatest ambition.

We cannot tell; there remains a real element of mystery about Keats's later work. Would he, if he had lived longer, have remained within the bounds of the purely aesthetic experience which had so far been most real to him: or would he have obeyed his continual prompting towards an interpretation of more general human experience: and is the latter an essential part of his nature, or is it simply a lingering relic of the endemic English puritanism, with its suspicion of non-utilitarian beauty? It is certainly the Keats of *La Belle Dame* and *The Eve of St. Agnes* who has produced the most numerous poetic progeny—the early Tennyson and the pre-Raphaelites being among them. The pre-Raphaelites indeed are his most obvious successors; and that, considering the narrowness of the pre-Raphaelite scope, is as much as to say that the work of Keats has never yet made its full impact on English poetry. Perhaps if he had reached maturity the pre-Raphaelite movement would have been a less abortive affair than it was, would have reached something of the dimensions of French symbolism. For myself, I find it easier to see him developing in this direction than towards the dramatic interpretation of life that he foresaw towards the end of his career.

In any case he has reached a further point of insight into the nature of the poet's problems than any other of the writers of his day. A whole new territory of poetic possibilities had been opened up by the romantic imagination. The rarity of complete and rounded achievement in Romantic verse, the fact that the Romantic poets "did not know enough", as Arnold complained, is accounted for by the extent and the difficulty of the country they were exploring. Coleridge had asserted the primacy of the imagination; but had shown only in a few brilliant flashes how it could combine the creative freedom of a dream with truth to some of the deepest facts of human experience. Wordsworth had exercised his power almost entirely on the bond between man and nature; and his strong grasp of the actual made him in many ways more akin to the eighteenth century than to the coming age. For the most part it was left to the second generation of Romantic poets to work out a relation between the actual and an imaginative ideal. Shelley leaves the dichotomy between the two almost unresolved. Byron frankly gives up the struggle and achieves his greatest successes on a lower level of insight altogether. It is to Keats if anyone that we must look for a solution of the Romantic conflict, and his solution is incomplete. And this is not merely due to the accident of an early death. It is impossible to say how much we have lost by the fact that the later Romantic poets died young—even Byron, the oldest, before the age at which we should expect an ordinary man of the world to reach his full powers. It is possible that we have not lost much, for Wordsworth and Coleridge too died young—as poets. It is in the nature of the romantic imagination that its achievements should be incomplete. It is also in the nature of human life; in spite of all the Horatian precepts,

> Be sure the reach of your own powers to know,
> How far your genius, taste and learning go

and all the rest of it, men do persist in attempting more than they can perform; and in some periods there is nothing else for them to do. It is possible to have an equal but different admiration for the classic who succeeds by knowing human limitations and the romantic who fails by trying to transcend them. We cannot now return to the uncritically accepted romantic dogma of the last century; but we need not be bamboozled by the rootless critical neo-classicism of the inter-war years. Mr. Eliot said in one of his earlier unguarded moments that there may be a place for romanticism in life, but there is no place for it in art. It was indeed necessary in the 'twenties to rehabilitate wit, intelligence and technical control; but there was surely something exaggerated and un-Augustan in the contemporary exaltation of the Augustan virtues; and those who felt that the Romantic poets were attempting something more than their immediate predecessors were after all right. There is no inevitable progress in the arts, but there is, as long as they remain alive, a continually growing tradition: and if we are to possess that tradition in our own age we must be prepared to absorb the romantic experience. There was a few years ago a real danger that the Romantic age would come to be regarded, as the eighteenth century once was before it, as an unfortunate interregnum in our poetic history. Keats's fragmentary lines to Fanny Brawne can bear a wider interpretation than their author intended. The Romantic movement does hold out a living hand to us, and not to grasp it is a kind of intellectual and emotional treason. We can perhaps see the results of the deliberate refusal of the romantic experience in this century in the present decay of creation, and the desiccation of much of our criticism. However much more final is our disillusionment with the actual world than any that was known to the Romantics, however much our historical experience exceeds theirs in painfulness and intensity, we have not in fact got far beyond their mode of interpretation. It is a mistake to tie up our wounds with the rags of Romanticism while denying the value of the whole cloth: and the difficult reabsorption of nineteenth-century values is one of the things that is needed for the mental health of the twentieth.

NOTES

Chapter V. Keats

1. *Keats, Letters*, ed. M. B. Forman (1935); I, 94.
2. ibid. I, 153.
3. ibid. I, 157.
4. Yeats, *Ego Dominus Tuus*.
5. The Greek influence on Keats has been vastly exaggerated. He neither knew nor cared anything about Greek history and civilization. He was fascinated by legend and mythology, and what he knew of Greek plastic art; but the world of Plato and the world of Pericles were alike closed to him. Besides Homer, transmitted *via* Chapman, the major influence at work is

the mythologizing Ovid. To regard this as representing Greece would be rather like omitting Goethe, Kant and Beethoven and representing Germany by Wagnerian opera and Grimm's fairy tales.

6. Sonnet: *On leaving some friends at an early hour.*

7. Letters, I, 156.

8. ibid. II, 426.

9. ibid. I, 273.

10. ibid. I, 154.

11. ibid. I, 103.

12. ibid. I, 112.

13. ibid. I, 245.

14. ibid. I, 77.

15. ibid. I, 74.

16. ibid. I, 281.

17. I had written this when I found a not quite similar but confirmatory suggestion in Ridley, *Keats' Craftsmanship*, p. 4: "I would suggest in passing that if in most places where Keats uses the word 'truth' (with its connotation of 'correspondence') we substitute the word 'reality', we are likely to come nearer to his meaning".

18. *v.* de Selincourt's edition of the Poems; M. Murry, *Keats and Shakespeare*; Ridley, *Keats' Craftsmanship*. Amy Lowell's biography is certainly wrong on this matter.

19. *v. Poems*, ed. de Selincourt, 487.

20. *Letters*, II, 419.

21. *Poems*, ed. de Selincourt, 486.

22. All this is not very different from what Mr. Murry is saying in *Keats and Shakespeare*: but he insists that the poem is finished, because the poet had at the time no more to say. I do not understand this use of the word "finished".

23. *Letters*, II, 149.

24. ibid. II, 419.

25. The status of this passage remains uncertain: *v.* de Selincourt, Murry and Ridley, who all discuss it.

26. *Letters*, II, 481.

A SHORT BIBLIOGRAPHY

GENERAL

T. M. Raysor (ed.), *The English Romantic Poets: a review of research* (New York, 1950, rev. 1956)

Oliver Elton, *A Survey of English Literature, 1780–1830* 2 vols. (1912)

M. H. Abrams (ed.), *English Romantic Poets: modern essays in criticism* (New York, 1960)

(Brings together in convenient form much of the good modern critical work.)

GRAY

Poetical Works, ed. A. L. Poole (Oxford, 1917, rev. F. Page, 1937)

Correspondence, ed. Paget Toynbee and Leonard Whibley 3 vols. (Oxford, 1935)

R. W. Ketton-Cremer, *Gray, a biography* (Cambridge, 1955)

Critical essays in *Johnson's Lives of the Poets* and *Matthew Arnold's Essays in Criticism*, 2nd Series

WORDSWORTH

Poetical Works, ed. E. de Selincourt and Helen Darbishire 5 vols. (Oxford, 1940–9)

Poetical Works, ed. John Morley (Globe Library, 1888, many reprints)

(Useful because it prints the poems in chronological order instead of in Wordsworth's own unhelpful arrangement; adds some valuable annotation.)

The Prelude, ed. E. de Selincourt (Oxford, 1926, 1932, rev. Helen Darbishire, 1959)

(1805 and 1850 versions on opposite pages.)

Mary Moorman, *Wordsworth, a biography* 2 vols. (Oxford, 1957–64)

Walter Raleigh, *Wordsworth* (1903)

John Jones, *The Egotistical Sublime* (1954)

F. W. Bateson, *Wordsworth: a re-interpretation* (1956)

Geoffrey H. Hartmann, *Wordsworth's Poetry, 1787–1814* (1964)

Critical essays in Matthew Arnold's *Essays in Criticism*, 2nd Series, and A. C. Bradley's *Oxford Lectures on Poetry* (1909)

COLERIDGE

Poetical Works, ed. E. H. Coleridge 2 vols. (Oxford, 1912)
Poetical Works, ed. J. Dykes Campbell (Globe Library, 1899, many reprints)
(Good biographical introduction and some valuable annotation.)
Biographia Literaria, ed. J. Shawcross 2 vols. (Oxford, 1900)
Biographia Literaria, ed. George Watson 2 vols. (Everyman, 1956)
John Livingstone Lowes, *The Road to Xanadu* (1927, 1930)
(The classic study of the sources of *The Ancient Mariner* and *Kubla Khan*.)
E. K. Chambers, *Coleridge, a biographical study* (Oxford, 1938, 1950)
Humphry House, *Coleridge* (1953)
George Watson, *Coleridge the poet* (1966)
Chapter on Coleridge in Basil Willey, *Nineteenth Century Studies* (1949)

BYRON

Works, ed. E. H. Coleridge and Rowland E. Prothero 13 vols. (1898–1904)
Poetical Works, ed. E. H. Coleridge (1905, many reprints)
Don Juan, ed. L. A. Marchand (1959) (Paperback, useful notes)
Leslie A. Marchand, *Byron, a biography* 3 vols. (New York, 1957)
Peter Quennell, *Byron, the years of fame* (1935)
Peter Quennell, *Byron in Italy* (1941)
Iris Origo, *The Last Attachment: Byron and Teresa Guiccioli* (1949)
Andrew Rutherford, *Byron, a critical study* (Edinburgh, 1961)
M. K. Joseph, *Byron the poet* (1964) (The most complete and thorough critical study.)
Critical essay by Matthew Arnold in *Essays in Criticism* 2nd Series
British Academy lecture, *Byron as poet*, by W. W. Robson (1957)

SHELLEY

Poetical Works, ed. Thomas Hutchinson (Oxford, 1905)
Letters, ed. R. Ingpen 2 vols. (1909)
Selected Poems, ed. John Holloway (1960) (Heinemann's Poetry Bookshelf; valuable critical introduction and notes.)
Newman Ivey White, *Shelley* 2 vols. (1940, 1947) (The standard life.)
Edmund Blunden, *Shelley, a life story* (1946)
Carlos Baker, *Shelley's Major Poetry* (Princeton, 1948)
K. N. Cameron, *The Young Shelley: genesis of a radical* (1950)

SHORT BIBLIOGRAPHY

KEATS

Poetical Works, ed. H. W. Garrod (Oxford, 1939, 1950)
Poems, ed. E. de Selincourt (1905, 1926) (Valuable critical introduction and notes.)
Letters, ed. Hyder Rollins 2 vols. (1958)
Walter J. Bate, *John Keats* (1963)
Aileen Ward, *John Keats: the making of a poet* (1963)
(These two lives, both excellent, came out in the same year.)
H. W. Garrod, *Keats* (Oxford, 1926, 1939)
J. Middleton Murry, *Studies in Keats* (Oxford, 1930; re-entitled *Keats*, and enlarged, 1955)
Robert Gittings, *Keats, the living year* (1954)
Robert Gittings, *John Keats* (1968)

INDEX OF WORKS DISCUSSED

A slumber did my spirit seal, 29
Adonais, 146
Aeolian Harp, The, 57, 66
Aids to Reflection, 93, 98
Alastor, 128
Ancient Mariner, The, 57 seq.
Anecdote for Fathers, 48
Animal Tranquillity and Decay, 44

Bard, The, 22
Beppo, 110
Biographia Literaria, 42, 75 seq.
Borderers, The, 41
Bride of Abydos, The, 104
Brothers, The, 44

Cain, 119
Cenci, The, 139
Childe Harold, 100, 106 seq.
Christabel, 65
Corsair, The, 104

Defence of Poetry, 150 seq.
Deformed Transformed, The, 119
Dejection, 57, 67
Descriptive Sketches, 32, 41
Don Juan, 111 seq.

Elegy in a Country Churchyard, 13 seq.
Endymion, 163 seq.
English Bards and Scotch Reviewers, 99
Epipsychidion, 148
Eve of St. Agnes, The, 167
Excursion, The, 87 seq., 98
Expostulation and Reply, 48

France: an Ode, 67
Frost at Midnight, 57, 66

Giaour, The, 104
Goody Blake and Harry Gill, 43
Guilt and Sorrow, 41

Hellas, 139
Hour of Idleness, 99
Hymn to Adversity, 12
Hyperion, 180 seq.
—— 2nd version, 187 seq.

I stood tiptoe upon a little hill, 159
Idiot Boy, The, 44
Intimations of Immortality, 55
Isabella, 166

Kubla Khan, 63

La Belle Dame Sans Merci, 169
Lamia, 167
Lara, 104
Leech Gatherer, The, 46
Lines Written in the Euganean Hills 141
'Lucy' poems, 29, 46
Lyrical Ballads, 41 seq.

Manfred, 108
Marino Faliero, 119
Michael, 44

Necessity of Atheism, The, 123

Ode to Autumn, 178
—— *on a Distant Prospect of Eton College*, 12
—— *to Duty*, 89
—— *on a Grecian Urn*, 176
—— *on Indolence*, 171
—— *to Liberty*, 140
—— *on Melancholy*, 177
—— *to Naples*, 140
—— *to a Nightingale*, 174
—— *to Psyche*, 172
—— *on the Spring*, 11
—— *to the West Wind*, 143
On First Looking into Chapman's Homer, 159
Ozymandias, 142

Political Justice, 38
Preface to *Lyrical Ballads*, 67 *seq.*
Prelude, The, 28 *seq.*
Progress of Poesy, The, 18
Prometheus Unbound, 133 *seq.*

Queen Mab, 124 *seq.*

Revolt of Islam, The, 131 *seq.*
Recluse, The, 85

S
Sardanapalus, 119
Sensitive Plant, The, 147
Sleep and Poetry, 161
Solitary Reaper, The, 46
Song at the Feast of Brougham Castle, 87
Sonnets of Wordsworth, 52
Strange fits of passion have I known, 48

Tables Turned, The, 48
This Lime Tree Bower, 66
Thorn, The, 44
Tintern Abbey, 29, 50
Triumph of Life, The, 149

V
Vision of Judgement, The, 118

We are Seven, 48
When the lamp is shattered, 142
White Doe of Rylsone, The 87
Witch of Atlas, The, 147